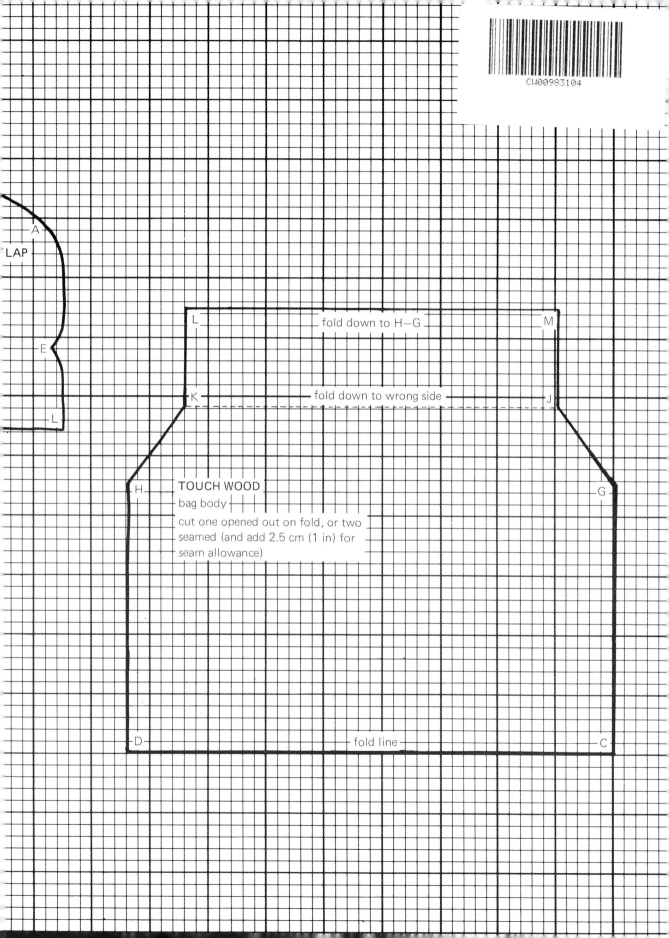

A
LAP
E
L

L — fold down to H—G — M

K — fold down to wrong side — J

H
G

**TOUCH WOOD**
bag body
cut one opened out on fold, or two
seamed (and add 2.5 cm (1 in) for
seam allowance)

D — fold line — C

# Fashion Bags

real leather

# Fashion Bags

real leather

## Eunice Wilson and Joanne Gale

B T BATSFORD LIMITED  LONDON

ISBN 0 7134 1073 6


Printed in Great Britain by
The Anchor Press Ltd., Tiptree, Essex
for the publishers B T Batsford Limited
4 Fitzhardinge Street London W1H 0AH

## ACKNOWLEDGMENT

People, companies and organisations have helped us greatly while we were
preparing this book. Our special thanks go to Jane Coveney, Brenda Mills
and the directors of Gomshall Tanneries whose enthusiasm and co-operation
made it possible. We are grateful, too, to Lesley Slight for the beautiful
examples of professionally-made handbags commissioned by the Pittard
Group of Companies, the photographs of which we have been allowed to
use. We should like to acknowledge the co-operation of the Leather
Institute for allowing us to use the international leathermark, and our
thanks also go to Mark Gerson for photographing the jacket illustration
and the colour plates specially for the book.
    We are also very much indebted to the following works of reference:
*Leather* by John Waterer; The British Leather Federation's *British Cowhide
Leathers*; as well as for information and historical illustrations from the
Leather Institute's *The Wonderful Story of Leather* by K.J. Beeby, and the
Northampton Museum of Leathercraft's *A Picture Book of Leather*.

4

# Contents

# Introduction

There was a time when the word 'leathercraft' conjured up visions of dark brown, thonged purses and handbags, or designs with intricate tooled patterning or complicated metal frames. And all seemed to be fashioned from the heaviest, stiffest of leathers with an array of lethal-looking tools.

Some of today's bags are quite as beautiful as some of the historical ones and this collection designed by Lesley Slight, one of Britain's leading handbag designers, for the Pittard Group proves it.

Particularly lovely is the Silver Jubilee leek, shamrock, thistle and rose design, finely appliquéd in silver and gold metallic leather onto clothing grain, with a belt to match (figure 1).

Delicate Oriental blossom or contrast stripes with embroidered edges are the themes for another striking pair of handbags and belts (figure 2). The style Jap (left) has a grain leather base with appliqué flowers of suede trimmed with snakeskin. The other style, Tudor, has quilted suede stripes with embroidered edges.

Figure 2

Luckily those days have gone. Today's meticulously refined leathers and suedes have the fineness and suppleness of silk. They come in colours, too, that are as exciting as they are unending: flamboyant pinks, purples ranging from African Violet shades to Victorian mauves, the green shades of lichen sharpening to the acid tones of lime, the pale and the indigo blues of denim, and the rustic shades of buttermilk, conker and acorn, forming a fashionable ethnic theme. The delectable icecream pastels have not been forgotten either, nor the flaunting extravagance of gold and silver kid.

Figure 1

As dye techniques and leather processing have become more varied and sophisticated, so fashion bag shapes have gradually softened and simplified, following fashion's unstructured path. In many cases, they have moved back through time to the practical shapes evolved by generations of peasant civilisations.

This general simplification of design has coincided with the rebirth of homecraft skills, bringing leather as a material well within the scope of the home-sewer as well as providing additional variety for those more experienced in leathercraft.

Now one can obtain skins that are as easy to work as fabric, and available to the amateur at a reasonable cost. The versatile collection of fun-but-practical bags provided here range from trendy mini moneybags to a striking flower satchel with a matching belt. The bags have been specially

Figure 3

designed for easy assembly, and complete sewing directions are provided for working in both suede and leather; a great many variations are also suggested to widen the choice. Some are so quick to make that you could finish them in an evening!

Leather is an extremely versatile material, and the possibilities for decoration are limitless. For instance, the different textures of leather and suede can be effectively contrasted. It is particularly good for patchwork, too, as it is firmer than fabric, as well as for appliqué motifs. Studding can be used as edgings or for more intricate patterns. Small wickerwork or coloured rush mats could make attractive panels. Stick-on beads can be formed into eye-catching designs or borders. Fancy knitting or crochet edging can easily be added also. From this first-ever fashioncraft bag collection, anyone with imagination can create designs with the stamp of their own creative flair.

Bold multi-colour stripes make another smart pair of matching fashion accessories in contrasting suede and leather, trimmed with scalloped and fancy zigzag embroidery by Lesley Slight (figure 3).

Finally, another exquisite example of fine machine embroidery, a spectacular orchid-style suede appliqué on a leather bag with a plainer toning belt. Also, in complete contrast, a multi-stripe pochette with a matching belt, again contrasting the textures of leather and suede (figure 4).

Figure 4

# Leather in our Lives

After the fig leaf, Eve's first body covering would have been fashioned from animal skins, so would the rough sleeping pallet she shared with Adam. She would have carried a shoulderbag, too, again made from skins, in which she placed berries and fruit, an important part of the daily diet.

Maybe it was only a crude circle of skin held together by thorns, perhaps with a drawstring of plaited grass, but it could well have been the first of the fashion bags as we have come to know them today.

Throughout history, the skins of animals, birds and reptiles have played an important part in everyday living. No one knows who used them first, but there is evidence that it was before the Ice Age. As well as killing and eating animals, the primitive peoples used the skins to protect their own bodies from the elements. To do this they needed to fashion tools with which to remove the remnants of flesh adhering to the inside of the skin after they had stripped it from the animal. Archaeologists have discovered crude types of scrapers, thought to be skin-scrapers. Some made from bone have been unearthed from Palaeolithic sites and others in iron or flint from excavations of later civilisations.

After scraping, men would probably have stretched out the skin to dry in the sun or the wind. The result would have been a skin that was not only hard and, therefore, difficult to keep wrapped round the body, but which chafed the human skin as well. The animal skins would also have disintegrated quickly as no one would have known how to preserve them or how to restore their initial suppleness.

Figure 5 Primitive man used a stone tool to scrape the skin

Gradually they would have learned to rub animal fats, often from the brain, into the skins to make them more pliable and easier to deal with. The Eskimos, to this day, soften skins by chewing, to the detriment of the teeth of their older women.

The putrefaction problem, though, still remained, and many centuries were to pass before man discovered tanning, the method of preserving the skin and turning it into leather as we know it today. Man probably stumbled upon the knowledge accidentally. Tannin or tannic acid, used in the tanning process, is obtained from the bark of oak or the more exotic sumac trees or seed pods. Perhaps some tannin was washed off a tree by the rain onto skins which had been thrown onto the ground below. From there, man would have learned to extract the tannin and mix it with water. This, he would have found, preserved the skins, and with his previous discovery that fats made them pliable, this would have been a major step forward.

At some time, no one quite knows when, someone would have discovered, probably again by accident, that a skin with the hair removed had even more uses. The most important of these was as a carrier for water, keeping it cool and fresh. This must have had a very great influence on the mobility of primitive tribes. It would have been no longer necessary to rely

Figure 6 The same action was used until modern times

Figure 7 Today chemicals are used to remove the hair

Figure 8 Leather fire bucket of the 17th century

on finding a water-hole wherever they wandered, a fact which would have encouraged them to start exploring far beyond their accepted territory. The suppler skins, too, would have resulted in more weatherproof living shelters or tents, some of which could be carried on their backs for long hunting expeditions.

These early peoples also learned to seam the skins together, judging from the remaining fragments of ancient clothing. First they made a series of holes with sharply pointed stones. Then they passed through them narrow strips of leather, a process which we have come to call thonging and overlacing.

Gradually over the centuries, man found increasing uses for the ever-finer leathers he was learning to produce from a growing variety of animal skins. From the early crude body coverings, leather, across the years, was fashioned into garments which were both practical and then, later, fashionable and luxurious. The hair was left on some of the more attractive skins and the first of the fine furs was evolved.

In the households of all except the poorest in the land, leather was used extensively for furniture and utensils, and also for working implements of all kinds. Leather also played a leading role in transportation, from the early primitive carts to the later horse litters, sedan chairs and coaches.

Leather carriers were no less important. They were used for wine as well as water, for meat or fruits, for coins, and for legal and ecclesiastical manuscripts. A tooled leather 'budget' or satchel, for example, was found in a ninth century Irish shrine. From the practical, they branched out to the more decorative, eventually establishing themselves firmly in the fashion scene as carriers of essential and frivolous 'appurtenances' for both men and women. A mercer in a thirteenth century French poem described his stock as including 'stamped purses of red, green and black' which he was to sell at fairs. In the seventeenth century, large purses made from chamoised goatskin segments with drawstring pockets were worn suspended from girdles.

Queen Berengaria, wife of Richard I, was recorded as distributing money to the poor from a soft drawstring bag suspended from her waist, called an *aulmonière*, or receptacle for alms (it is from this that the word 'almoner' has evolved). Purses were equally important in Chaucer's day for he included one in his description of the young wife in his *Miller's Tale*:

'And by her girdle hung a purse of leather
Tasselled with silk . . . .'

A sumptuous purse of crimson satin, embroidered with gold, was among Henry VIII's inventory of Greenwich Palace.

Knights, too, paid their dues by flinging down small drawstring leather purses filled with gold coins. Even to the present day, boxers are still rewarded 'by the purse'. The pursuits of hunting and hawking, as well, called for special pouches or bags. These were often made from *cuir bouilli* leather boiled in oil to make it especially hard and durable. An early sixteenth century German purse for a huntsman is described as having thirteen pockets and compartments, some of them secret. It also has a frame of wrought iron with innumerable catches and loops by which it

Figure 9 Leather-covered coffer of the
16th century

Figure 10 Leather wine flask of the 17th
century

Figure 11 Leather-covered sedan chair of
the 18th century

was attached to a belt, which made it extremely heavy and cumbersome
to wear.

Then there were the handsewn leather fire buckets used after the time
of the Great Fire of London. They were both practical and decorative, and
could well have provided the inspiration for the bucket-shaped fashion
bags of the 1940s. The ornamental leather-covered caskets from medieval
times onwards, too, were without doubt, the forerunners of today's vanity
cases.

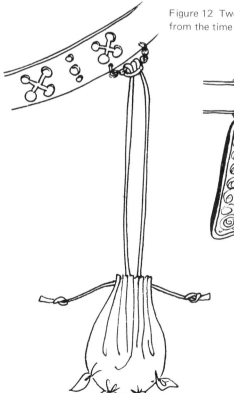

Figure 12 Twelfth-century aulmonière
from the time of Richard I

Figure 13 Gipcière of cuir bouilli

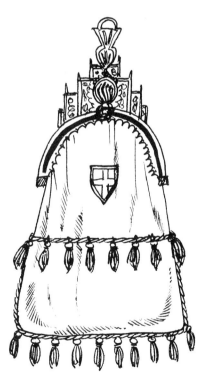

Figure 14 Gipcière of the 15th century

13

Figure 15  Chatelaine belt of 1550

Figure 16  Waist purse of 1880

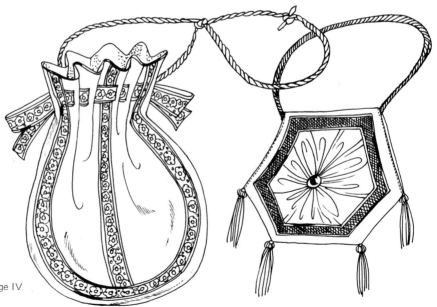

Figure 17  Purses from the time of
George I (c 1720) and (*right*) George IV
(c 1825)

# Looking at Leather

## SKINS AND THE WAY THEY ARE PROCESSED

Leather is the skin of an animal from which both the hair and remaining shreds of flesh have been removed, chemically and mechanically, by the tanner. The skins are then tanned in a combination of liquids which changes the remaining gelatinous-like substance into a sheet of long, tough, intricately-woven leather fibres. This is then dressed, or curried to use an older term, a process which consists of washing, oiling, stretching, softening, colouring, polishing and embossing.

The term 'skin' usually refers to that which comes from sheep, lamb or goat. Those of beef animals, however, are called hides. These are too thick and heavy for most purposes and are, therefore, split into two layers as shown in figure 18. The split hide, or top hair-bearing layer, is punctured all over with miniscule holes (follicles) from which the hair once grew, and has very short fibres which form a fine crust called the grain. The hide split or meat side, on the other hand, has long, loosely-woven fibres with no grain. After splitting, the hides are tanned and dressed as for skins but, during the latter process, an artificial grain is given to the top surface of the hide split. It is, however, not as well-defined as a natural one.

Leather in its natural state is a very light brown colour, so full-grain hides are often finished with a sole transparent aniline stain before being polished to give a high-gloss finish. This accentuates the graduations of natural colours and grain variations most attractively.

Another pleasing finish is hand-boarding which softens the leather still further and, at the same time, brings up a pattern of hairlike wrinkles to the surface without changing the colour or textural variations.

To produce a variety of colourings other than the natural shade obtained from aniline staining, the leather is given a light or heavy coating of pigment or 'dope' as it is sometimes called. The colouring comes in a fine powder form which is suspended in a suitable adhesive. After being treated with pigment, the leather is then finished in the same way as after aniline staining.

Damaged grain surfaces often have the outer surface 'snuffed off' with emery. Providing this is done lightly, the hide can then be finished with aniline stain or pigment and the result is almost indistinguishable from a normal full-grain hide. The characteristic skin pores and grain variations are less obvious and the leather is not so abrasion-resistant.

Where the damage to a hide is even more severe, the grain can be removed by deep buffing. A heavy coat of pigment will be required afterwards, and this is often 'fixed' by a coating of lacquer. This results in a surface which is uniformly level, but devoid of full-grain markings.

The hide split also has to be pigment-treated and finished with lacquer. This leather is quite serviceable but the surface is less resistant to constant rubbing and the hide is, therefore, sold at a lower price.

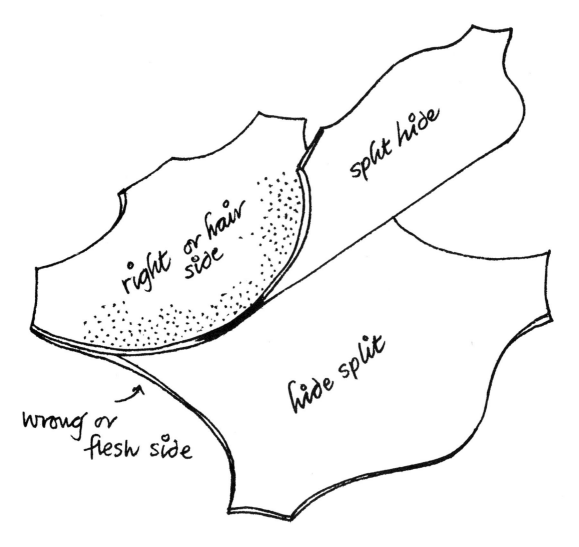

right or hair side

split hide

hide split

wrong or flesh side

Figure 18  The two layers of a hide

Both the split hides and hide splits can be embossed with a variety of grains or patterns, often a simulation of reptile, exotic animal or bird skins. This has no detrimental effect on the leather and gives creative people a more interesting and exciting range of surface effects with which to work.

WHICH SKIN TO CHOOSE?

Clothing leathers are the most suitable category for the type of fashion bags featured in this book. The leather comes mostly from sheep or beef animals, and the suede from lamb or goat.

Sheepskins are the most widely used because of their versatility. The skins vary widely in thickness and have a good surface which drapes well. Sometimes, of course, the wool is left on for making up sheepskin coats or jerkins.

Lambs and goats have skins of finer texture. Each skin has an inside and outside and when the finishing process is carried out on the outer, or grain, side, the leather is known as nappa. If, however, the finishing takes place on the inside of the skin, the resultant rougher-surfaced leather is called suede.

The splits from beef animals are cheaper than sheepskins and, therefore, are the best for the beginner to start with. At the other end of the quality scale are calf and kid, producing leathers of the finest quality and, consequently, higher prices.

Bear in mind when making your decision that the more pouched the bag design, the softer the skin it will require. Larger bags, on the other hand, will be firmer in a thicker skin. Explain clearly what you intend to make when ordering, and leave it to the leather supplier to produce the appropriate skins.

SUEDE is a fine clothing leather with a velvety nap or pile which comes in a wide variety of bright or pastel fashion colours. Choose it preferably for a bag that is not going to be used every day.

WASHABLE SUEDE is ideal for everyday bags, beachbags or family carry-alls. It washes perfectly if the washing instructions which accompany each skin are followed exactly.

GRAIN LEATHER, also referred to as smooth, glacé or nappa, comes in several weights or thicknesses, so be sure to ask for the soft, pliable variety only.

BARGAIN BUNDLES, consisting of suede or grain leather pieces, can be useful for motifs, patchwork, handles, drawstrings, fringing or thonging at the lowest possible cost.

## SIZES AND GRADES OF SKINS

Skins, like the animals from which they come, vary in size, but the type usually available has an area of roughly 5,574 sq cm (6 sq ft), or 76 x 61 cm (30 x 24 in).

Although they are put into the same dye vat, batches tend to vary slightly in colour (as with knitting wools). Therefore be sure you buy sufficient leather before starting to make up a bag, otherwise it will be difficult to match the exact colour later.

The processing of skins is uniform, but they do vary in quality and are graded according to the amount of skin that is usable. Grade 1 denotes a skin the whole of which is good quality. Grade 2 will have a good, but less perfect finish. Grade 3 has a greater number of mainly natural flaws derived from the animal rubbing against posts or fences, or a blow from another's horns or butting head.

It is safer, therefore, to buy Grade 1 skins for all but the smaller bag designs like Miss Moneybags, Puffills or Jazz up a Hat-and-Scarf set. The Kingsize Bag and luggage-size version of the Jaunty Duffle, though, will require more than one skin.

Grade 3 can be used as a lining leather, unless the leather supplier can offer a lower-grade skin for that purpose. Be careful not to use a non-washable lining leather on a washable suede bag. If, on the other hand, you prefer a fabric lining, avoid the iron-on kind. When heat is applied, skins expand, and when they cool again they contract to their original size, invariably causing the interfacing to wrinkle. Try, too, to use a non-fray interlining so that the edges which are not turned in do not look ragged.

## THE WORKING SHAPE

The hide or skin of an animal is divided into four main parts as shown in figure 19. The best-quality leather comes from the butt section which has the closest-woven fibres, and this is, therefore, the best section from which to cut the main part of the bag design.

The second best part of the hide is the shoulder, but this usually has wrinkles or long growth marks. Therefore, unless the bag design is the type which natural marks would enhance, it is best to avoid cutting into this area for the main bag shape.

The neck and two belly sections have the loosest weave fibre, particularly in the armpit areas. The leather is usually even more creased than the shoulder, and should be kept for gussets and linings, or any other parts of the pattern which will not show.

Figure 19  The working shape

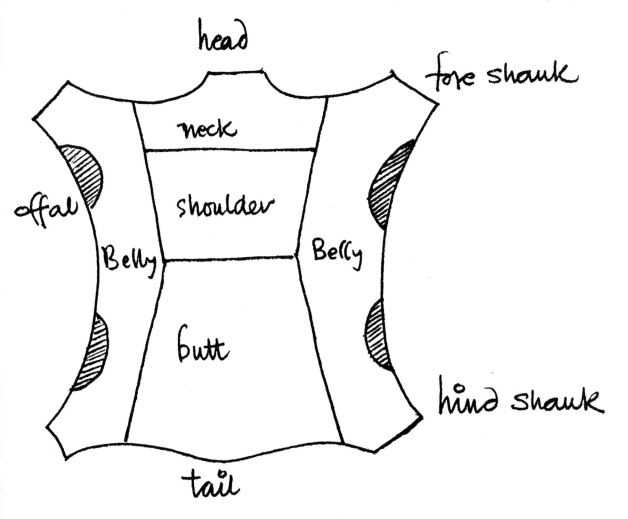

# Tools and Equipment

### SCISSORS AND KNIFE

Two types of scissors are necessary. A 20 cm (8 in) flat-bottomed pair is required for cutting out large leather pieces, and a small, straight-bladed manicure-type pair is needed for fringing and other fine cutting.

Although skins can be cut quite easily with scissors, it is useful to have a sharp craft knife as well, as this is more efficient when cutting along straight edges (using a steel ruler as a guide).

### HAND-SEWING NEEDLES

Tailor's short needles which neither bend nor break during use are best for staystitching and reach places where the sewing machine cannot function. Number 7 is suitable for sewing a single layer or two thin layers, and Number 3 is the best size for sewing several thicknesses at a time.

### THONGING NEEDLES

A crewel needle with a blunt end, or, for careful workers, an extra-large darning needle, can be used for this purpose. It would be worthwhile, however, to buy a spring thonging needle which is split at the eye end.

### PUNCH PLIERS

The revolving sixway type is the most generally useful, as it can punch six different hole sizes through any thickness of leather.

### EYELETS

These have a hand tool for closing them into the punch holes. Eyelets come in brass or coloured metal finishes, and in sizes from 200 to 700.

### A RIVETER

If the tabbed fastening method is to be used, a hand-riveter will be necessary.

### RIVETS

These come in various metal finishes and in a range of sizes.

## STITCH MARKER

A wooden-handled wheel marking 8 or 10 stitches to 2.5 cm (1 in) is a useful addition to any tool collection.

## RULERS

A steel ruler is the best kind to use as it does not slide about on the skins and it cannot be sliced through by a cutting knife. A wooden school ruler on which the common degree angles (including 45°) are marked is another asset.

If you intend to become an expert in working with leather, it is worthwhile to acquire a professional curved ruler also. Otherwise, use dinner plates, LP discs and other curved objects to draw larger curves, and coins, wineglasses or saucers for smaller ones.

## A PAIR OF COMPASSES

These are for drawing cardboard circles in the Dashing Dollybag version with handles.

## ADHESIVES

Use the adhesive recommended by the leather supplier. The following brands are also suitable for use on leather: Copydex, Evostik Impact, Magic Crystal Clear Cement, UHU, Urethane Bond (UK): DuPont Duco Cement, Ross Plastic Cement, Elmer's Glue-All (USA).

## PATTERN PAPER

Use squared pattern paper marked with 5 cm (2 in) squares, each divided into 1 cm ($^3/_8$ in) squares, such as Dewhurst's paper No. S 298, or Chartwell True Sew paper No. 1902.

## TAILOR'S CHALK

This is white and should be used to mark patterns and points on the wrong side of the skin. It is easily brushed off the skin after use.

## PAPERCLIPS

These are a substitute for tacking stitches and must, therefore, be large enough to hold edges or leather shapes together firmly, without being so tight as to make a permanent mark on the skin.

# Basic Techniques

## USING THE SEWING MACHINE

Use a size 14 needle in the sewing machine for single-thickness skins. Where there are several layers of leather to deal with, size 16 or even 18 will be necessary. A thread with natural fibres (such as Sylko) is best. Synthetic threads tend to slip and do not 'give' with the pull of the leather. Always use the largest stitch on your sewing machine, with six stitches to 2.5 cm (1 in).

Ease the pressure on the needle bar which takes the weight off the foot so that the teeth do not cut into the skin and tear it as it is being sewn. Feed the skin, firmly but gently, under the foot of the machine; never attempt to pull it through.

## PRESSING

Skins can be pressed quite safely with a *dry* iron, on a silk setting, if the iron is kept moving all the time. Never use a pressing cloth, or lint from it will be pressed into the skin and this will be extremely difficult to remove. Brown paper can be safely used instead.

After machining darts or seams, press the seam open by running the thumb along the stitching line. Then lightly stick down the underside of the turnings and press on the wrong side.

## ASSEMBLING THE PATTERN

A beginner with leather would be well advised first to cut and make up the design for a bag in cheap calico, or material taken from a discarded cotton dress, until a degree of confidence is reached. The patterns in this book were worked out on Chartwell True Sew dressmaker squared pattern paper No. 1902. This has heavy lines forming 5 cm (2 in) squares, each divided into 1 cm ($^3/_8$ in) squares.

Mark the measurements on points corresponding to the scaled-down pattern on the end papers of this book; join the points with a pencilled line, then cut out the pattern and paperclip it to the material or leather.

For patterns which need to be used several times, make a template of the shape in stiff card or a durable interlining material such as Vilene.

## CONVERSION MEASUREMENTS

The measurements in this book have been worked out individually in metric and imperial. In many instances, the measurements given will not be accurate conversions of each other (this is done to avoid having awkward sizes). Therefore the reader can use either one system or the other, but not both on the same article, as they are not interchangeable.

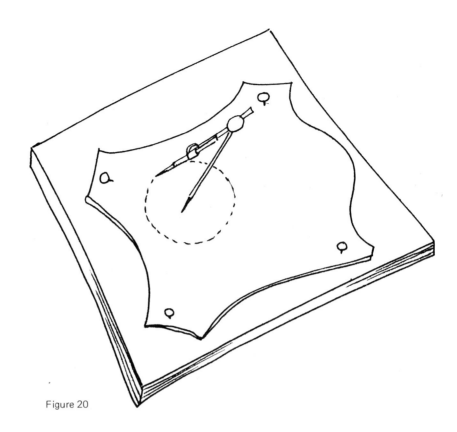

Figure 20

## TIPS FOR THE PROFESSIONAL TOUCH

(1)  Skins are a great deal easier to mark a pattern on and cut out if they are first pinned to a flat board with drawing-pins, thumb tacks or map pins (figure 20).

(2)  Always lay the pattern pieces on the leather so that they run down the grain of the skin, from neck to butt.

(3)  Place the pattern pieces to the smooth side of the skin as there are generally fewer flaws to be avoided.

(4)  Mark the pattern on the flesh side of the skin with tailor's or ordinary blackboard chalk, as this does not permanently mark the skin.

(5)  Never using tacking stitches as these will leave unsightly holes in the leather. Instead hold the skins together with long paperclips which can be removed, one by one, as machining progresses. Alternatively, using masking or clear adhesive tape.

(6)  Always stick zips onto the wrong side of the bag with a leather adhesive before machining. This ensures that the zip is kept in place while stitching, and strengthens the zip opening.

(7)  After sticking down edges which are about to be seamed, always leave them to dry before stitching, otherwise the adhesive will clog the machine needle and thread.

(8)  To make machining near the edge easier, cut one of the pieces a

larger size and allow its surplus to stick out underneath the edge of the other. This surplus can be trimmed away when machining is completed

(9) Make cardboard templates of applied motifs so that you can make use of them several times, particularly on matching accessories.

Figure 21

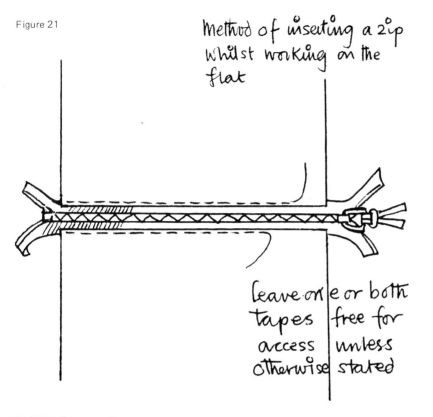

Method of inserting a zip whilst working on the flat

Leave one or both tapes free for access unless otherwise stated

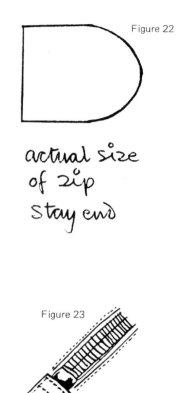

Figure 22

actual size of zip stay end

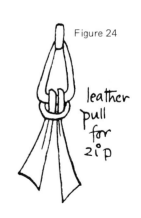

Figure 23

leather tag for stay end of zip

Figure 24

leather pull for zip

## PUTTING IN A ZIP

Working flat (as shown), lay both bag shapes, right sides downwards, on the zip tape with the straight edges facing one another (figure 21). Using a suitable adhesive, stick the zip between them with 2.5 cm (1 in) of its length projecting at each end. Leave to dry. Turn the bag over to the right side and stitch the zip into position, using a zip foot attachment on the sewing machine if you have one. If sewing by hand, use a stitch marker to ensure that all the stitches are exactly equal.

Trace the actual-size pattern for the zip stay end off the page (figure 22), place the pattern against the leather, and cut out. Attach this tab to the right side of the bag, stitching it onto the end of the tape projection (figure 23). Finally, knot a thonging loop onto the zip pull (figure 24).

## MAKING LEATHER THONGS

Thongs can be bought in pre-cut lengths from a leather supplier, or they can be cut from a skin using a craft knife and a steel ruler. Do not cut them narrower than 3 mm ($\frac{1}{8}$ in) or they may break under tension.

Thongs can be used to hold two pieces of leather together permanently in the form of a seam, or as a fastening device for an opening. Thonging can also be used as a form of overcasting along an edge, such as the flap on the front of a bag, to strengthen and decorate it.

To calculate the amount of thonging required, measure three times the length of the punched edges. The holes should be made with punch pliers, and the thongs can be threaded with a crewel needle or a spring thonging needle. Always test-punch any hole for size first on a spare piece of leather. Ideally, thonging should thread through the hole easily but without room to slip about. Never force it through a hole that is too small, or the leather will tear.

## DECORATIVE THONGING

A new dimension can be added to thonging by beading or fine fashion-type chain loops. The latter can be bought by the metre (yard) from good haberdashery departments. It can also be cut into the required lengths with ordinary electrical flex cutters.

For the beading variations shown in figure 25, thread each bead onto the thonging strip before pulling it through the punch hole.

Figure 26 shows how the chain is attached. The thonging is threaded through the loop of the chain before it is passed through the punch hole. The process is then repeated with loops of equal length along the edge to be overlaced.

For plain overlace thonging see figure 119, page 84.

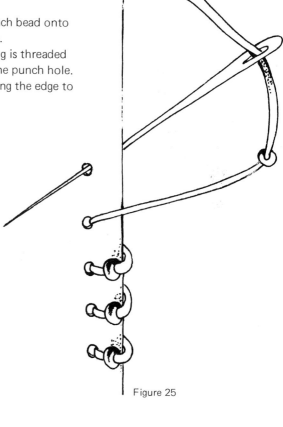

Figure 25

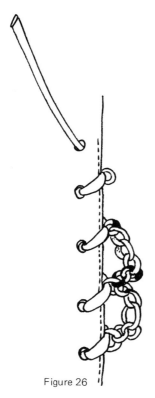

Figure 26

## THONGING USED TO JOIN EDGES

If you prefer to thong the edges of a bag without gluing or stitching, first tie the punched edges together with thread in at least three places to hold them firmly as illustrated (figure 27), so that the punch holes line up exactly. The tacking threads can be cut away after thonging is completed.

For hand-staystitching to reinforce corners, double-thread the needle as illustrated, as this makes the stitching far stronger.

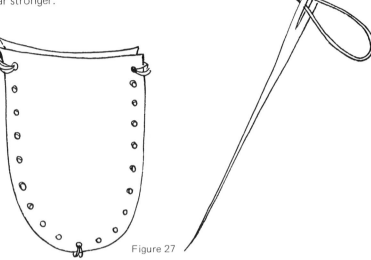

Figure 27

## MAKING A SEAM

The two parts of the bag can be placed wrong sides together and machine stitched round the edge. To strengthen the seam, stick the edges and allow them to dry before machining. This kind of seam can be made more decorative by inserting a zigzag strip between the two parts before they are joined, as shown (figure 28).

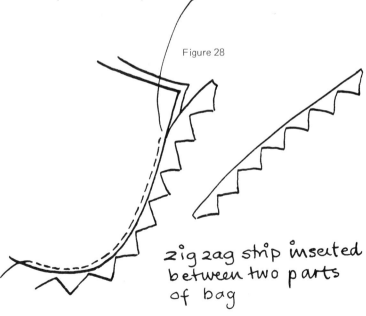

Figure 28

zig zag strip inserted
between two parts
of bag

To cut a regular zigzag, mark off equal lengths along one edge of the strip with chalk, then draw a parallel line a short way in from the edge and mark off the same equal lengths along the line, but staggered to fall half-way in between the other marks. Join up all the marks to give the zigzag shape, then cut along it using a craft knife and steel ruler. It is best to experiment with a zigzag strip in paper first to arrive at a shape which will suit the size of the bag.

Alternatively, a plain seam can be made by placing the two parts of the bag right sides together, machining 6 mm (¼ in) or more in from the edge, and turning the bag right side out so that the machining lies on the inside. Again, gluing the seam beforehand will make it stronger.

This seam can be decorated with thonging. Punch the holes for the thonging before the seam is made up, by placing the parts of leather together and punching through both thicknesses; this will ensure that they align on either side of the seam when it is joined together. The holes should appear as groups of four, so that the thonging can be crossed in an attractive pattern as it is laced through (figure 29).

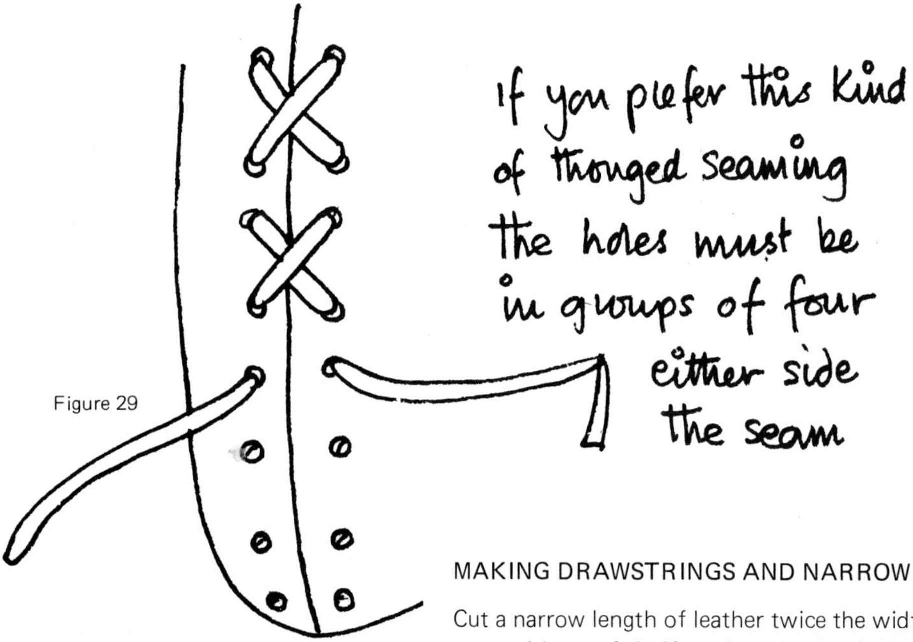

Figure 29

*If you prefer this kind of thonged seaming the holes must be in groups of four either side the seam*

## MAKING DRAWSTRINGS AND NARROW STRAPS

Cut a narrow length of leather twice the width required for the finished strap with a craft knife and steel ruler, fold it over down its length, and press lightly with a dry iron. Machine stitch down one side to hold the two thicknesses together. This double thickness of leather is stronger than a single thong, and does not stretch so easily, and it can therefore be used as both a drawstring and a carrying strap. The ends can be fringed by cutting with the knife, and may be knotted, or a small strip of leather may be tied round the end to act as a stop (figure 30).

If the strip of leather available is not long enough to make the draw-string in one piece, two lengths may be joined together. Cut the two ends to be joined on a slant corresponding with each other, spread adhesive over the surface and between the two ends, then fold the leather over as normal and stitch across the join. Since the ends are at a slant, the top part of one end will be stitched to the bottom part of the other end.

The drawstring may be attached to the bag by being passed through decorative metal rings sewn to the outside of the top opening. Alternatively it may be threaded through holes punched in the top edge of the bag which should be protected from tearing by the insertion of metal eyelets.

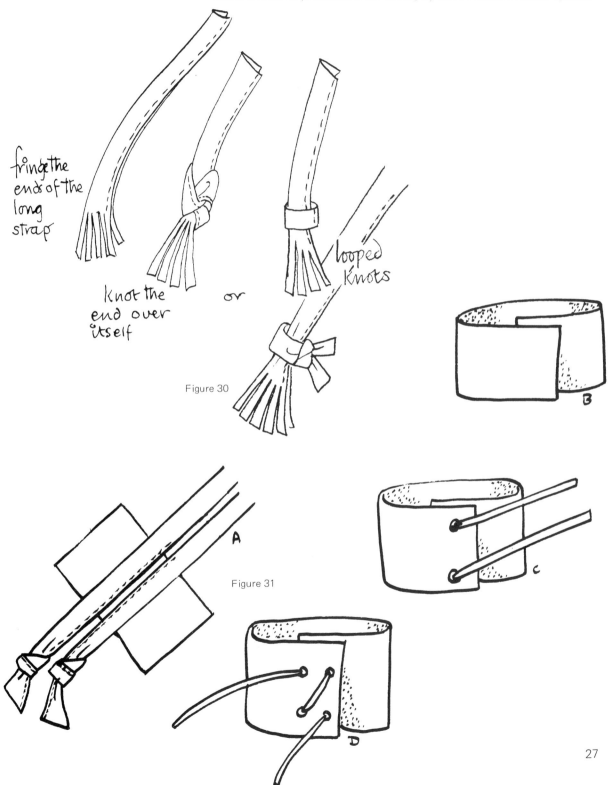

fringe the end of the long strap

knot the end over itself

or

looped knots

Figure 30

Figure 31

27

## MAKING DRAWSTRING STOPS

Cut out a small rectangle of leather 19 mm (¾ in) wide, with the length twice the combined width of two thongs laying side by side, plus 2.5 cm (1 in) extra for the overlap as shown in A (figure 31). Overlap the short ends and stick down as shown in B. The ends can be stapled as well for extra reinforcement.

Alternatively, punch the ends with two or four holes as shown in C, and lace them together with narrow thonging as shown in D. Push the drawstring down through the stop, and draw up the neck of the bag.

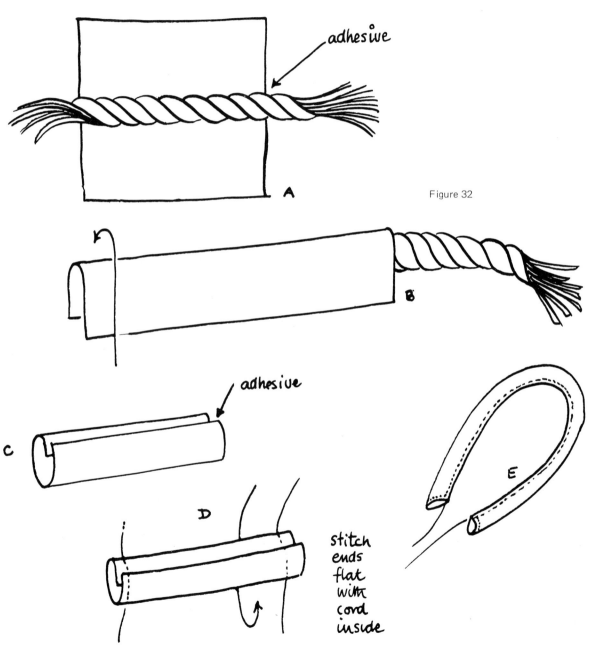

Figure 32

## MAKING LEATHER HANDLES

On the wrong side of the leather strip, lay a piece of piping cord centrally along the length as shown in A (figure 32). Stick, and leave to dry. Fold over the leather so that it covers the cord to within 6 mm (¼ in) at either end as shown in B. Repeat this procedure for the other strip. Leave to dry, then stitch as shown in E.

Alternatively, roll the strip over the cord as for a rouleau in dressmaking, as shown in C, D and E, and then stick together. Handsew along the joined edge, leaving the ends open, or whipstitch the edges.

## MAKING A CHAIN HANDLE

Decorative chain can be bought by the metre (yard) from good haberdashery departments to make attractive handles. When choosing chain for the handle, be sure to pick one with strong links and not one of the lighter, purely decorative ones. Remember that the handles must be glued and stitched in position *before* the bag is seamed at the sides.

Holding the bag where you will want it to hang, measure, with a piece of string, the length either of a shoulder strap or a carrying handle. Then cut an identical length of chain with electrical flex cutters. Next cut two strips of leather, twice as wide as the inside width of one of the links, and 10 cm (4 in) in length. Fold the strip edge, centre to centre, on the wrong side as shown (figure 33). Stick down and leave to dry. Thread a strip through either end of the chain and stick the ends together.

Figure 33

Mark lightly with chalk on the back of the bag two fixing points 13 mm (½ in) in from either side, and the same distance down from the flap fold of a clutch bag design. Stick the glued handle ends onto these points and leave under a heavy weight to dry.

Finally with a No. 16 or 18 needle in the sewing machine, and the pressure on the needle bar eased to take the weight off the foot, machine in an oblong as shown.

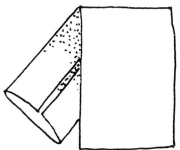

Always remember to cover the ends of a metal chain with leather before attaching them to the bag to prevent the metal from cutting into the leather.

## MAKING A PLAITED HANDLE

Measure the length required using a piece of string, then add an extra 5 cm (2 in) to the length of the strip, as the plaiting will shorten the length by about this amount. Divide the strip into three, and mark two inner points as shown (figure 34), 3 cm (1½ in) down from the top edge. Then cut with a knife two lines up to these points using a metal ruler as a guide. Place strip 1 as shown. Place strip 3 under strip 2, and continue plaiting, or braiding, in the normal way. Be sure to pull the braiding fairly tightly as you proceed, smoothing it out at intervals to keep it flat.

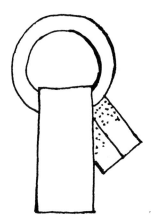

When the plaiting is finished, line up the three ends and cover them with adhesive tape to prevent the braid from slipping undone. Using paperclips, fasten the braid in position for machining, but before stitching, remove the adhesive tape, otherwise it will clog the needle.

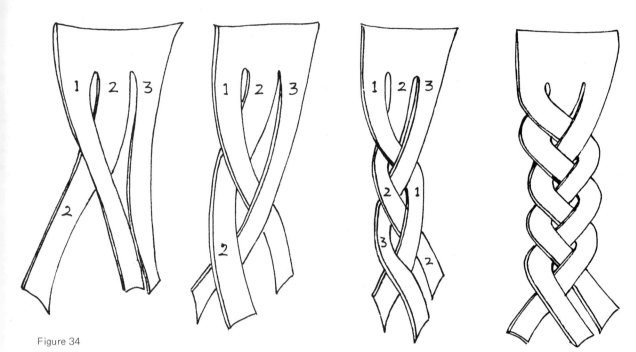

Figure 34

Figure 35

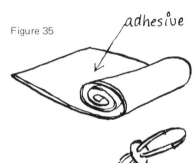

adhesive

## MAKING LEATHER FASTENERS

For the leather button, cut a strip of leather 3 x 10 cm (1½ x 4 in). Spread adhesive over the whole of its inside surface, then roll it up as shown until it forms a solid tube (figure 35). Leave it to dry.

Next punch a hole through the centre of the tube. Thread a two-holed dressmaker's button or bead onto strong button thread and push the two ends through the hole. Alternatively, punch two holes through the rolled up tube, thread a narrow leather thong through the holes and pull it up tight.

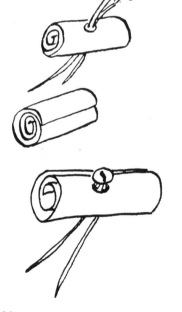

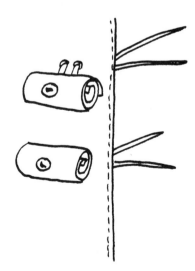

Holding the leather roll firmly, pass the thread ends through punched holes on the bag from the outside. On the wrong side, pull the ends tight so that the roll rests firmly against the bag; knot, and finish off.

Finally, again on the wrong side of the bag, stick a small square of leather over the thread ends so that they cannot work loose. Leave to dry.

If you prefer to tie thonging round the button rather than punch holes through it, wrap the thonging round it several times to hold if firmly (figure 36a). For a toggle fastening, make the loop as shown (figure 36b).

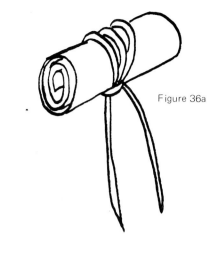

Figure 36a

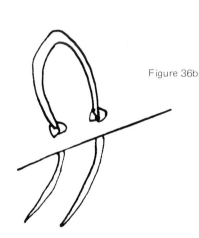

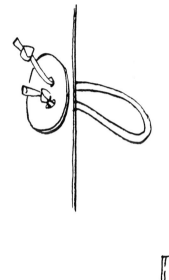

Figure 36b

## MAKING A TABBED FASTENING

Flapover bags can be fastened, if preferred, by extending the lower edge of the flap into a long tongue with a rounded end. Its width should be in proportion to the size of the bag. This tongue should then be lined with lining leather.

Cut a tab strip (under which the tongue will be pushed) long enough to allow sufficient room for the rivet strips, which will hold it to the bag (figure 37). Round off the corners of each end of this strip. Back it with lining leather. Stitch the ends in a figure D as shown onto the bag.

Next cut two small narrow strips which will hold down the tab strip, and line them with fabric lining. Rivet them to the bag body as shown.

alternative tab shape
held down by bar
under rivetted strips

Figure 37

attachment stitching
at either end.

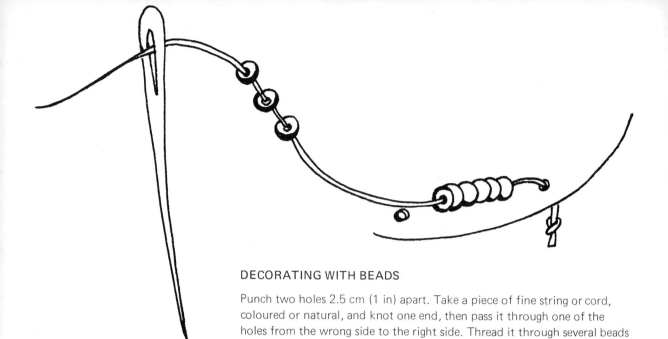

## DECORATING WITH BEADS

Punch two holes 2.5 cm (1 in) apart. Take a piece of fine string or cord, coloured or natural, and knot one end, then pass it through one of the holes from the wrong side to the right side. Thread it through several beads and push them down towards the hole (figure 38).

Figure 38

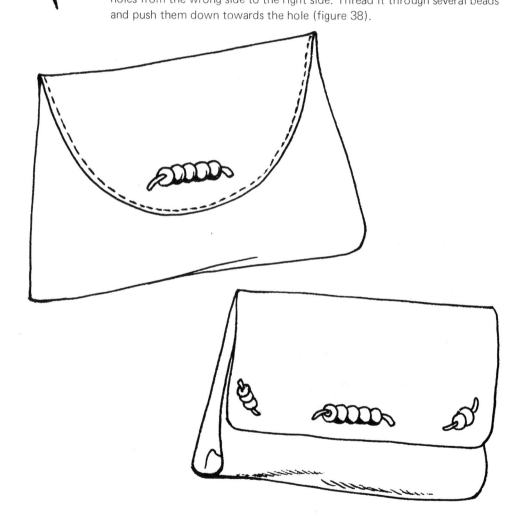

Then thread the string through the eye of a large needle and push it through the other hole from the right side to the wrong side. Draw it up tight, and knot off securely on the wrong side. If a longer row of beads is preferred, knot the string between each bead.

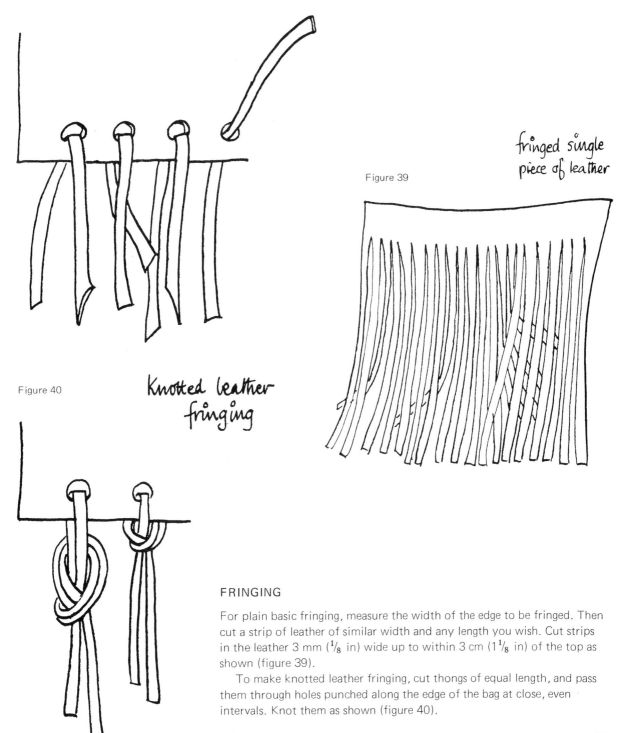

Figure 39

fringed single piece of leather

Figure 40

Knotted leather fringing

## FRINGING

For plain basic fringing, measure the width of the edge to be fringed. Then cut a strip of leather of similar width and any length you wish. Cut strips in the leather 3 mm ($\frac{1}{8}$ in) wide up to within 3 cm ($1\frac{1}{8}$ in) of the top as shown (figure 39).

To make knotted leather fringing, cut thongs of equal length, and pass them through holes punched along the edge of the bag at close, even intervals. Knot them as shown (figure 40).

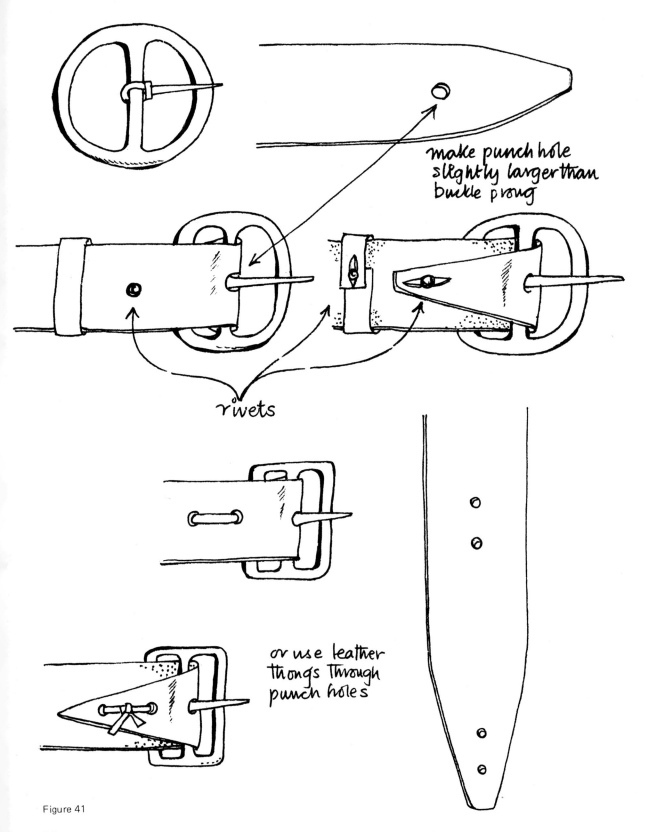

make punch hole
slightly larger than
buckle prong

rivets

or use leather
thongs through
punch holes

Figure 41

34

## MAKING A BUCKLE FOR A SHOULDER STRAP

Buckles are readily available from haberdashery stores, and are sold in a range of shapes and sizes. By adding a buckle to a shoulder strap you can make it adjustable, and add a professional look to the bag. Cut the straps in one continuous piece of leather or suede, the same width, wide enough to pass through the buckle comfortably, and long enough to overlap each other by about 5 cm (2 in) or more. If a single thickness of leather is not strong enough to carry the weight of the bag, glue two thicknesses together and machine stitch them as close to the edges as possible, to make some really sturdy straps. Attach the two bottom ends to the outside of the bag by stitching or riveting, then taper the top ends by cutting with a craft knife.

On one strap, punch about four holes in a line, large enough to take the prong of the buckle; these are for adjusting the length of the straps when in use. On the other strap, punch just one hole, slightly larger than the prong to allow it to move backwards and forwards, and push the prong through it, then double back the tapered end of the strap onto the wrong side of the leather. Fasten it there with a rivet, or with a thong threaded through two holes and tied as shown (figure 41). Do not use stitching to secure it as this will not be strong enough to take the strain.

Finally, place a small strip of leather round the strap a little way along from the buckle, and fasten it at the back with a rivet. This must be just loose enough to allow the end of the other strap to be threaded through it after being passed through the buckle.

# Miss Moneybags

Made in an evening, these top-fashion mini moneybags are worked in soft, fine leather, and need no stitching. Carry in them coins for meters, telephones, taxis or American 'mad' money . . . keys . . . make-up . . . or other vital bits and pieces.

Figure 42

2.5 cm

13 mm (½ in)

actu
of
pu
grad
fr

*Tie them round your waist*

*slot them through your sleeves*

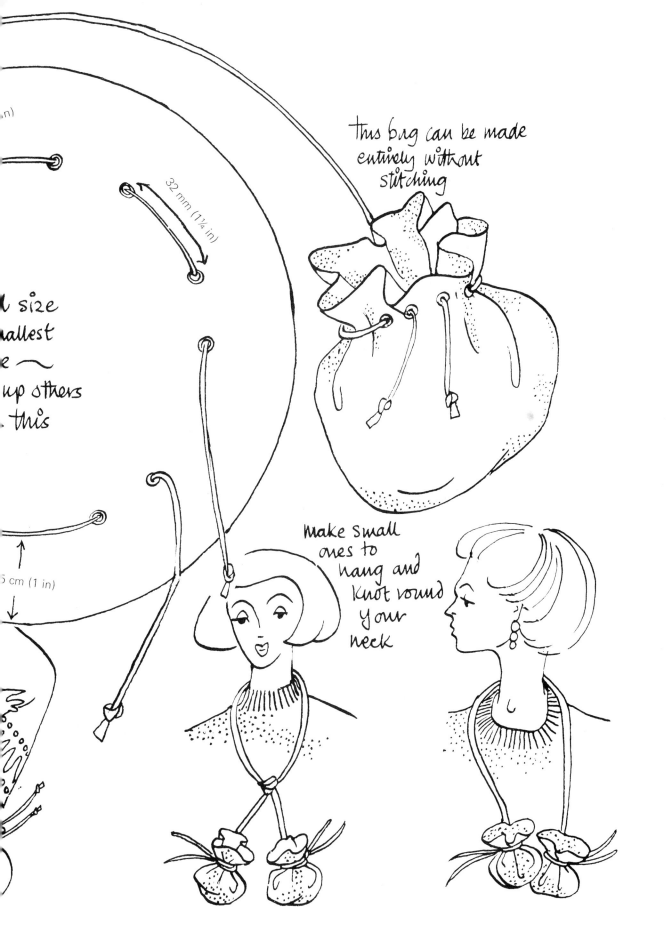

This bag can be made entirely without stitching

32 mm (1¼ in)

...l size
...mallest
...e ~
...up others
...this

...5 cm (1 in)

Make small ones to hang and knot round your neck

Sling them round your neck — in pairs or clusters. Thread them through sleeves like a child's gloves. Or tie them low round your hip chatelaine-fashion.

Grouped in sizes they are even more fun. Make some as gifts, too, for your friends — and you will go straight to the top of the popularity poll!

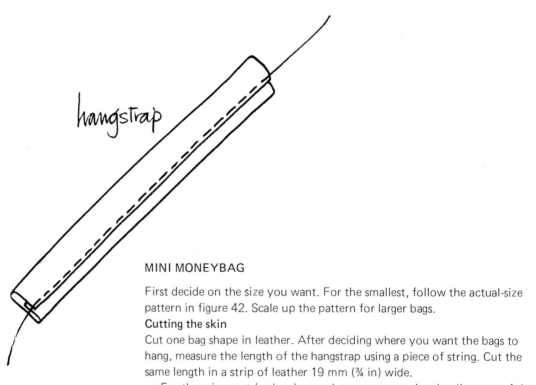

hangstrap

Figure 43

## MINI MONEYBAG

First decide on the size you want. For the smallest, follow the actual-size pattern in figure 42. Scale up the pattern for larger bags.

**Cutting the skin**

Cut one bag shape in leather. After deciding where you want the bags to hang, measure the length of the hangstrap using a piece of string. Cut the same length in a strip of leather 19 mm (¾ in) wide.

   For thonging, cut (or buy) enough to measure twice the diameter of the eyelet circle line, following the directions in Puffills on page 84.

**Preliminary assembly**

Make the hangstrap as in figure 43, folding it in three to form a form a 6 mm (¼ in) wide strip. Stick, leave to dry, and stitch. Alternatively use plaited thonging.

**Making up**

STEP 1.   Mark about twelve punch holes 2.5 cm (1 in) in from the outer edge on the main circle marking the four main punch holes with a pair of compasses before marking the rest. Insert eyelets to protect the holes from tearing both at 13 and 32 mm (½ and 1¼ in) intervals as shown in the pattern.

STEP 2.   Attach the hangstrap ends to the outside of the bag just below the drawstring on the *opposite* side to the knotted ends. Stick and leave to dry. Machine a double row of stitching, or stitch in a square for maximum holding strength.

STEP 3.   Thread the thonging through the eyelets, and knot off the ends on the outside of the bag, or thread with a bead. Draw up the thonging and tie in a bow.

## INITIALLED MONEYBAG

### Cutting the skin

Cut one circle in leather, and another circle 13 mm (½ in) larger in lining leather, to make the multi-rows easier to stitch close to the edge. Cut one or two initials in leather as in figure 44.

### Making up

STEP 1.   Stick the initial on the bag front. Leave to dry, then stitch round the edges to ensure that they stay flat.

STEP 2.   Stick the inside of the lining to the inside of the leather circle. Leave to dry. Machine round the outer edge with several rows of stitching, then cut off the surplus lining leather.

STEP 3.   Punch and thong the bag as in the previous version, attaching the hangstrap if required.

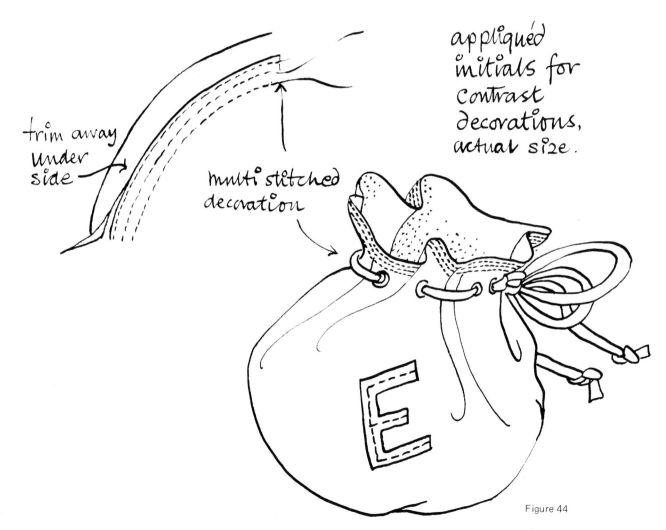

trim away
under
side

multi stitched
decoration

appliqued
initials for
contrast
decorations,
actual size.

Figure 44

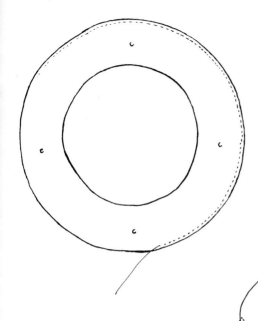

If it is neccesary to stiffen the gathered top of the bag, a lining may be stitched or glued in. Mark the four main punch-holes before making the rest

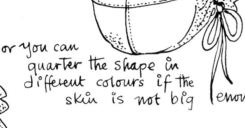

or you can quarter the shape in different colours if the skin is not big enough.

or add circles to firm up the base

or you can tape the seams with a contrasting strip

## MONEYBAG VARIATIONS

If it is necessary to stiffen the gathered top of the bag, a lining may be stitched or glued in. One or two small circles may also be stitched onto the outside at the bottom to firm up the base.

If the skin is not large enough to cut out the shape in one piece, divide the pattern into quarters, and cut it out from different coloured skins where possible.

If using the same coloured leather, tape over the seams with a strip in a contrasting colour (figure 45).

Figure 45

40

# Jazz up a Hat-and-Scarf Set

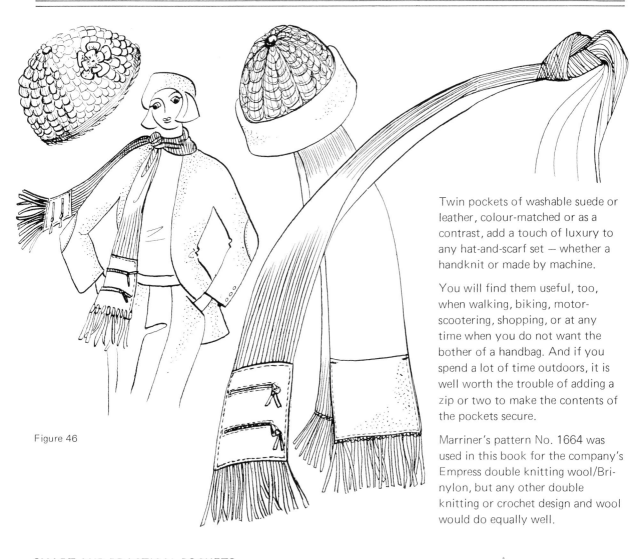

Figure 46

Twin pockets of washable suede or leather, colour-matched or as a contrast, add a touch of luxury to any hat-and-scarf set — whether a handknit or made by machine.

You will find them useful, too, when walking, biking, motor-scootering, shopping, or at any time when you do not want the bother of a handbag. And if you spend a lot of time outdoors, it is well worth the trouble of adding a zip or two to make the contents of the pockets secure.

Marriner's pattern No. 1664 was used in this book for the company's Empress double knitting wool/Bri-nylon, but any other double knitting or crochet design and wool would do equally well.

## SMART AND PRACTICAL POCKETS

Figure 47 is an actual-size pattern, but before tracing it off the page check the width of the scarf as differing crochet or knitting tensions can alter the sizing. Draw a square the same size, but add 2.5 cm (1 in) along the top and 13 mm (½ in) along the bottom and the side for the turnover. Then cut two pocket shapes in *washable* leather.

### Making up
STEP 1.   Holding the pocket with the wrong side towards you, stick down the 2.5 cm (1 in) turnover along the top and the 13 mm (½ in) allowance round both the sides and the bottom. Leave to dry, ensuring that the adhesive does not lie in the folds where it will be stitched.

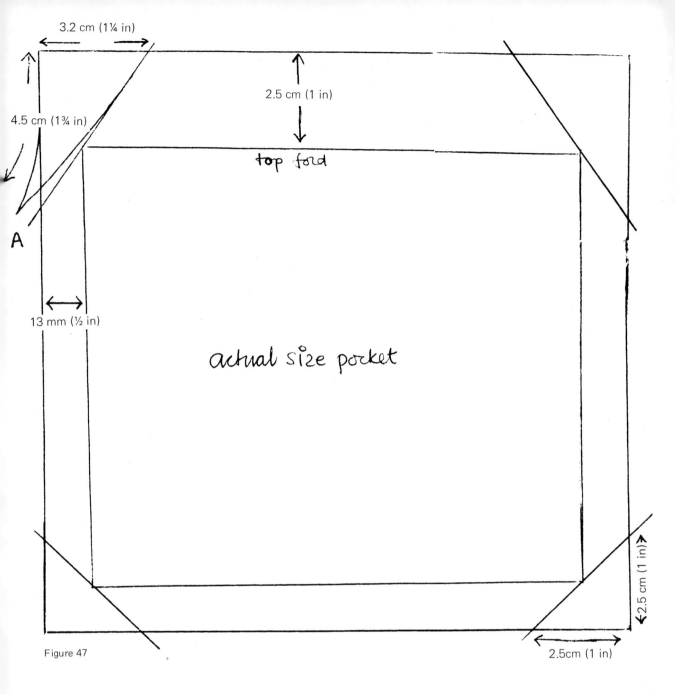

3.2 cm (1¼ in)

2.5 cm (1 in)

4.5 cm (1¾ in)

top fold

A

13 mm (½ in)

actual size pocket

2.5 cm (1 in)

Figure 47

2.5cm (1 in)

STEP 2.   Cut off all four corners as shown in figure 47, then place the wrong side of the pocket on the scarf above the fringe. Anchor it in place with paperclips.

STEP 3.   On the leather **not** the crochet side of the work, machine along the sides and the bottom 6 mm (¼ in) in from the edge. Reinforce the two opening corners with hand-staystitching. Repeat this method for the other pocket.

If you wish the pockets to be zipped, elongate the pattern and follow the zip insertion instructions on page 23.

# A FUN FLOWER FOR THE HAT

## Pattern preparing

Using the actual-size patterns in figure 48, cut five large petal shapes B, 4 smaller petal shapes D, and two base shapes A. Fringe the edge of one of them as shown in G.

## Making up

STEP 1.   Dart the base of each petal B as shown in F. Stick and then press flat. Next stick the petals onto one of the circles A as shown in C. Then stick the petals D on top of the larger ones, as shown in E.

STEP 2.   Punch two holes on either side of the centre G and the corresponding base A.

STEP 3.   Stick the fringed circle onto the middle of E covering the flower centres. Leave to dry.

STEP 4.   Next attach a bead, as shown in H, through the punched holes. Finally sew the flower onto the cap, remembering to place a folded square of ribbon or tape on the wrong side of the crochet to give the stitches a firm anchorage.

Figure 49

Figure 48

A, B and D, are actual size

more pocket ideas

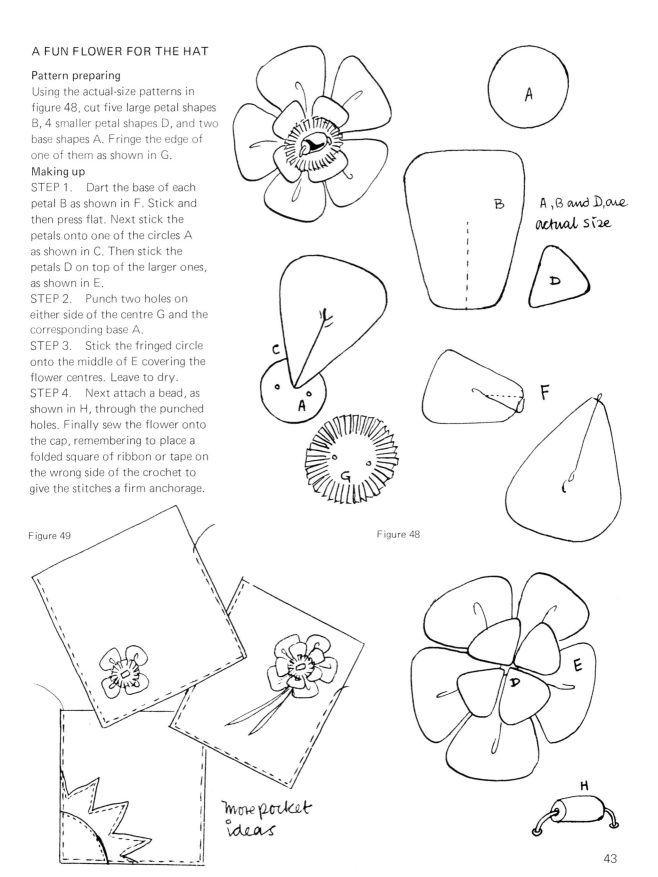

43

# Jaunty Duffle

Duffle bags are part of everyone's lifestyle today — from nursery school upwards. Dashing designs, though, are not all that easy to find, so why not make one yourself that will turn heads?

The basic pattern is simple enough for a novice to tackle, and you can ring the changes with very little extra effort. Patched . . . fringed . . . thonged . . . or fancy-yoked, these go-anywhere practical bags appeal to everyone from six to sixty.

Figure 50

## THE LARGE VERSION

### Skin requirements

For the larger version you are likely to need two skins. If you want to be more economical and use just one, cut the large oblong into two equal pieces but add 2.5 cm (1 in) to each half piece measurement to allow for the two 13 mm (½ in) seam allowances.

### Pattern preparing

For the large luggage-size version, draw round an LP disc for the base and cut round it. Next cut an oblong for the bag body 45 cm (18 in) wide, and cut the length to equal the circumference of the base plus 2.5 cm (1 in). Then cut another oblong the same length, but only 7.5 cm (3 in) wide, to reinforce the bag top.

### Cutting the skin

Cut the base shapes, one in leather, one in lining leather and a third, 13 mm (½ in) smaller, in cardboard or side leather to reinforce the base. Cut one body oblong in leather. Cut the 7.5 cm (3 in) eyelet strip in leather.

### Preliminary assembly

Apply any fancy motifs or panels while the bag is flat. Make eyelet holes along the top body edge 3 cm (1½ in) down from the top and about 5 cm (2 in) apart, but spacing them so that the holes straddle the main seam. Make a *firm* thong following the directions on page 23, and drawstring stop as on page 28.

### Making up

STEP 1.    With the right sides of the bag body together, stick the ends A together (figure 51). Leave to dry, then stitch. Press open the seam and stick flat. Leave to dry.

STEP 2.    Again with the right sides together, stick the ends of the 7.5 cm (3 in) strip together. Leave to dry. Stitch, press open the seam and stick flat. Leave to dry.

STEP 3.    Stick the wrong side of the eyelet strip to the right side of the bag body, overlaying its bottom edge by 13 mm (½ in) onto the top edge of the body. Stick and stitch as shown in figure 52 making sure the two joining seams are not lined up over each other.

STEP 4.    Attach the base to the body as shown in figure 53. Leave to dry, then stitch together 13 mm (½ in) in from the edge, easing in carefully as you go. Finally notch the base seam with sharp scissors to allow it to 'sit' properly.

Figure 51

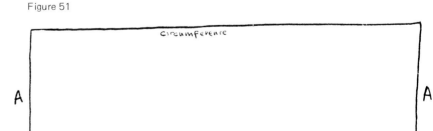

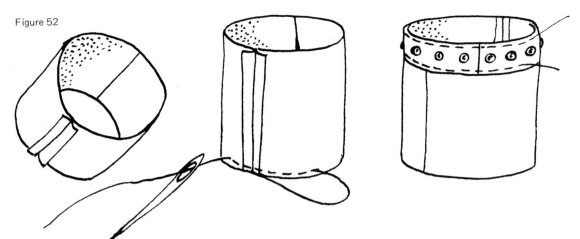

Figure 52

STEP 5.    Turn the bag right side out and place it upright on a flat surface. Fold over the sides so that you can reach inside. Flatten out the circular seam. Then spread adhesive over the base and underside of the seam turnback nearest to it. Next place the cardboard base onto the leather base, so that it slips under the glued seam turnback. Press down and leave to dry. Stick the lining base on top of it and leave to dry.

STEP 6.    Thread the thonging through the eyelets and knot or fringe the ends. Draw up the neck of the bag to complete.

## THE SMALL VERSION

For a smaller version, use the actual size circle in Puffills on page 83 for the base, decide on the height you want, then follow the method of working given above.

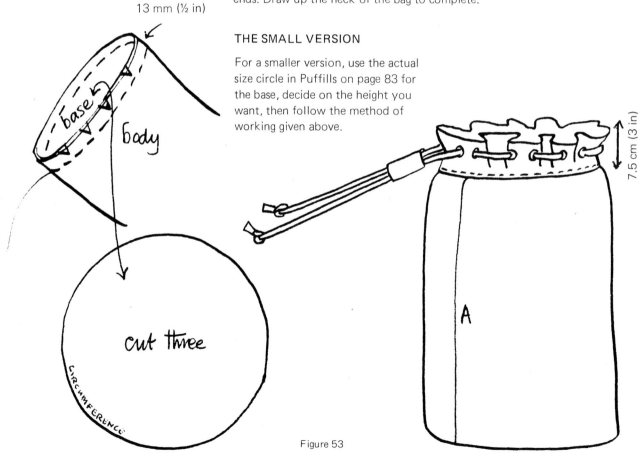

13 mm (½ in)

base

body

cut three

CIRCUMFERENCE

7.5 cm (3 in)

A

Figure 53

# Fun Flowers

Add a touch of colour and luxury to a bag . . . a cloche hat . . . a jerkin . . . clogs . . . or fashion boots.

Make them in different sizes, singly or in clusters. Or make up your own more elaborate multi-layer variations.

### STAR FLOWER

First draw a circle on paper, using the actual-size pattern (figure 54) and cut it out. Next mark the inner circle which is 19 mm (¾ in) smaller. Then cut points round the outer edge of the circle A, but avoid cutting into the inner circle line. Make the petals irregular to add more life to the shape. Finally place the paper pattern on the skin, and cut out the pointed-edge shape in leather.

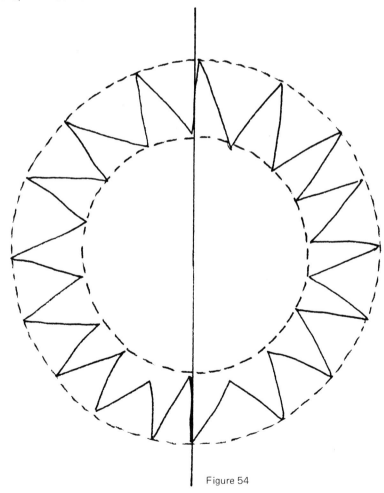

Figure 54

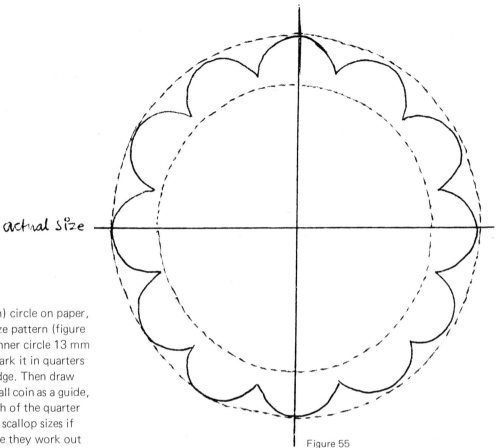

actual size

Figure 55

## DAISY FLOWER

Draw a 10 cm (4 in) circle on paper, using the actual-size pattern (figure 55), and mark an inner circle 13 mm (½ in) in depth. Mark it in quarters round the outer edge. Then draw scallops using a small coin as a guide, and starting at each of the quarter points. Adjust the scallop sizes if necessary to ensure they work out exactly.

Cut round the main scalloped paper shape and place the paper pattern on the skin. Then cut out the shape in leather. Repeat this in diminishing sizes using coins and the end of a pencil as guides. Then glue the layers one on top of the other. Finally finish off with a bead in the centre.

## FLOWER VARIATIONS

The flowers can be decorated, and at the same time attached to the garment or accessory, by beading and thonging. Using a needle to make two holes, string one large or several small beads onto strong thread, and secure with a knot. If using thonging, punch four holes, thread the thonging through, and finish off as shown (figure 56).

The flowers can be as varied as desired, and the star and daisy shapes can be combined into one flower. By cutting individual petal shapes and gluing them in place, using different coloured leather, attractive three-dimensional flowers can be built up (figure 57).

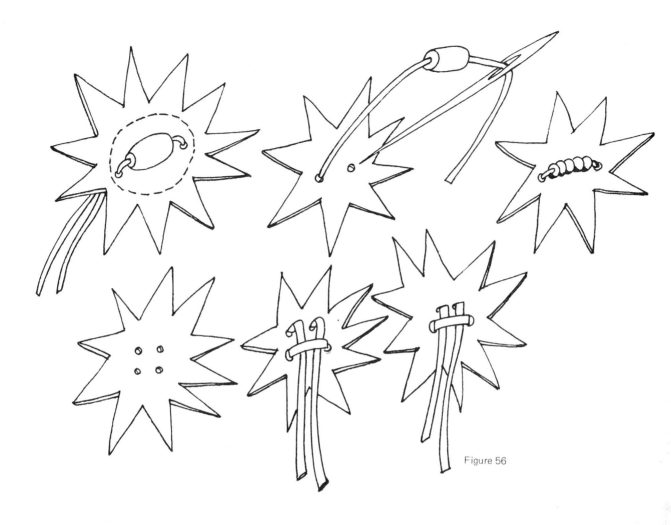

Figure 56

Figure 57

49

## TIED BUTTON FLOWER

A very simple flower shape can be made by placing a square of leather over a button, and tying the leather to it with thread as shown (figure 58). Four small petals can be glued onto the basic square shape to form a very attractive flower.

This flower can be used to decorate any of the bag designs in this book. By attaching the button firmly to the bag first, the flower does not need to be secured with any further stitching when it has been constructed (figure 59).

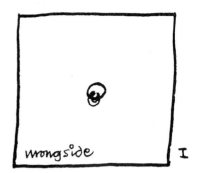

*wrong side*    I

Figure 58

Figure 59

use the tied flower motif
for another bag

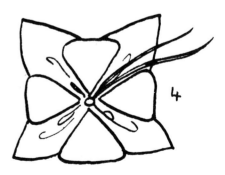

*right side*    3

4

*stick petals on to right side*

50

# Fashionably Patched

Patchwork has undergone a revival and is now in the forefront of fashion. The leather version is particularly striking, and its firmness makes it a lot easier to put together than cotton fabric.

Even a beginner can tackle this attractive bag design whether it is to be plain, have a panel of patches, or to be patchwork all over with a plain flap fastener.

Figure 60

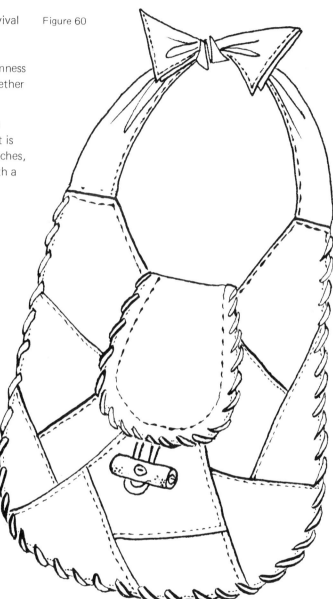

## THE BASIC SHAPE

### Pattern preparing
Cut one basic bag shape (on which the patches are to be mounted) in paper, following the pattern on the back end papers of this book. Cut one flap as shown in the pattern.

## Cutting the skin

Using the paper pattern, cut two bag shapes in leather, and two more in lining leather, calico or lining material 6 mm (¼ in) smaller all round. Cut one flap in leather, and one in lining. Cut two handle strips 35.5 x 10 cm (14 x 4 in). Cut a 10 cm (4 in) length of thonging for the handle loop.

## Preliminary assembly

STEP 1.   Stick the thonging loop to the wrong side of the flap with adhesive, inserting both ends to a depth of 2.5 cm (1 in) as shown in figure 61. Then, with the wrong sides together, stick the lining to the flap. Leave to dry, and stitch round the sides and the front over the loop ends.

STEP 2.   Punch holes round all but the flap back, 6 mm (¼ in) inside the edge stitching, 13 mm (1½ in) centre to centre. Overlace with thonging. Make a further row of stitching *outside* the overlacing, both for decoration and to anchor the loop firmly in place as shown in figure 61.

STEP 3.   With the wrong sides together, fold each of the two handle strips in half lengthways. Stitch round the three open sides as shown in figure 62.

STEP 4.   Stick the lining to the front bag body, leaving a 6 mm (¼ in) surplus all round. Leave to dry. Do not stitch together yet. Repeat for the back.

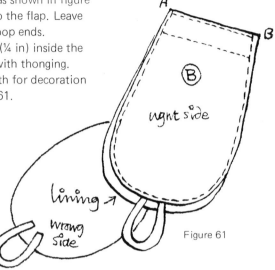

insert leather loop into flap before attaching to back of bag opening

A
B
Ⓑ
right side
lining →
wrong side
Figure 61

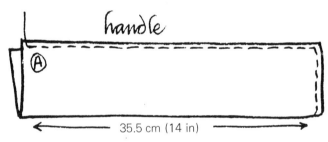

handle

Ⓐ

35.5 cm (14 in)

Figure 62

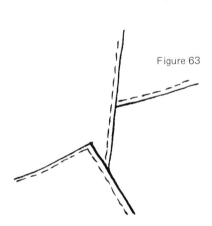

Figure 63

## SIMPLE PATCHWORK

### Topstitching overlaid patches

Cut small patches in fancy but simple shapes as shown (figure 63), all roughly the same size. Stick the wrong sides to the right sides of the bag front and back, ensuring that no more than two complete edges overlap. Also take care that the adhesive does not run over the edges.

When the adhesive is dry, machine each shape onto the bag front and back. Trim off any surplus patch leather along the edges.

### Zigzag stitching butted patches

A zigzag stitch attachment on the sewing machine will enable the patches to be joined together decoratively as shown in figure 64. The patches should be butted, not overlapped, and must therefore fit tightly like a jigsaw puzzle.

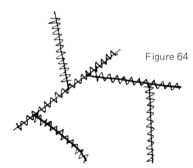

Figure 64

## MAKING THE PATCHWORK BAG

### Making up

STEP 1.   With the wrong sides together, place the front and back bag shapes  together. Insert the handle strips at the shoulders E–C and E–D, as shown in figure 65a. Stick them down, secure them together with paperclips, and leave to dry.

Stitch two lines across the shoulder 6 mm (¼ in) apart. A larger needle and stitch will ensure being able to stitch through the three layers. Fasten the handle ends together temporarily with paperclips (later they will be knotted).

STEP 2.   Stick the wrong side of the A–B to the right side of the bag body at Z–Y–Z. Paperclip them together and leave to dry. Machine a double row of stitching along Z–Y–Z or make an oblong as shown in figure 65b. If the layers should turn out to be too thick, stitch them by hand.

STEP 3.   With the back and front bag shapes held together with paperclips at C–G–H–H–G–D, (see pattern), stick the 6 mm (¼ in) surplus together and stitch.

STEP 4.   Punch holes, 13 mm (½ in) apart, round this edge, 6 mm (¼ in) within the stitching line (figure 66).

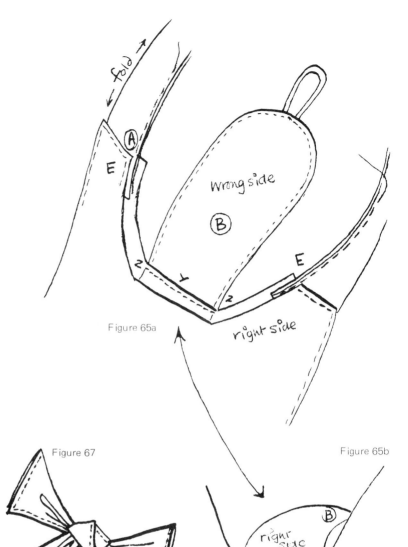

Figure 65a

Figure 65b

Figure 67

Figure 66

punch and interlace after stitching bag pieces together

STEP 5.   Stitch along the single raw edges of the bag opening E–Z and Z–E on the bag back and front.

STEP 6.   Make a rolled leather button as shown in the instructions on page 30. Mark its eventual position on the bag front using the loop fastener as a guide. Attach it there.

STEP 7.   Overlace the bag sides with thonging, and tuck in the thong ends neatly.

STEP 8.   Knot off the handle ends as shown in figure 67.

53

# Huntsman's Pouch

This simple-to-make pattern gives you a pouch bag echoing the swagger of the huntsman if you add a shoulderstrap or slot it through a belt.

If, on the other hand, you prefer the ageless look of classic elegance, make the contrast flap in suede, satin, velvet, corduroy, or any other fashion fabric. You can also embroider it, or punch intricate patterns on it.

One thing you can be sure of — it will team effortlessly with flouncing skirts or jeans, skintight or flared.

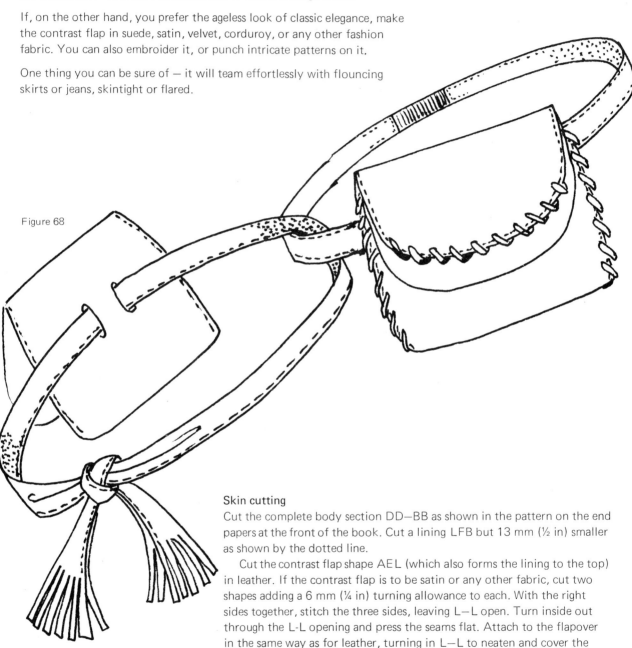

Figure 68

### Skin cutting

Cut the complete body section DD—BB as shown in the pattern on the end papers at the front of the book. Cut a lining LFB but 13 mm (½ in) smaller as shown by the dotted line.

Cut the contrast flap shape AEL (which also forms the lining to the top) in leather. If the contrast flap is to be satin or any other fabric, cut two shapes adding a 6 mm (¼ in) turning allowance to each. With the right sides together, stitch the three sides, leaving L—L open. Turn inside out through the L-L opening and press the seams flat. Attach to the flapover in the same way as for leather, turning in L—L to neaten and cover the lining edge inside.

54

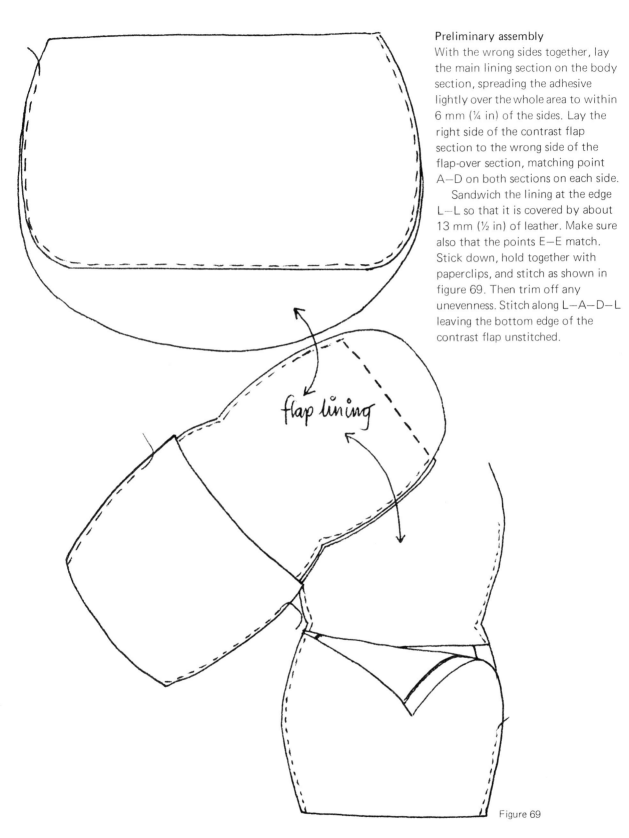

**Preliminary assembly**

With the wrong sides together, lay the main lining section on the body section, spreading the adhesive lightly over the whole area to within 6 mm (¼ in) of the sides. Lay the right side of the contrast flap section to the wrong side of the flap-over section, matching point A—D on both sections on each side.

Sandwich the lining at the edge L—L so that it is covered by about 13 mm (½ in) of leather. Make sure also that the points E—E match. Stick down, hold together with paperclips, and stitch as shown in figure 69. Then trim off any unevenness. Stitch along L—A—D—L leaving the bottom edge of the contrast flap unstitched.

flap lining

Figure 69

55

**Making up**

STEP 1:   With the wrong sides together, fold the pouch at F-F. Stick the
6 mm (¼ in) surplus at the sides B-F together. Make sure the lining is stuck
firmly along B-C-B as it is to be left unstitched. Anchor with paperclips,
leave to dry and stitch. This makes the pocket. Trim off any unevenness.

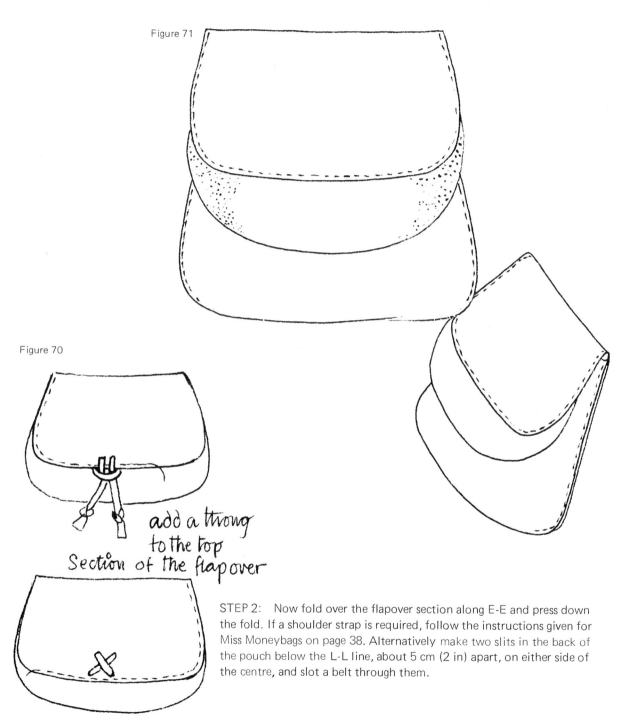

Figure 71

Figure 70

add a thong
to the top
Section of the flapover

STEP 2:   Now fold over the flapover section along E-E and press down
the fold. If a shoulder strap is required, follow the instructions given for
Miss Moneybags on page 38. Alternatively make two slits in the back of
the pouch below the L-L line, about 5 cm (2 in) apart, on either side of
the centre, and slot a belt through them.

# Casual Carryall

Peasant-braided . . . decorated
with initials or other motifs . . .
studded . . . fringed . . . or merely
left plain, this simple but effective
design will take you fashionably
anywhere.

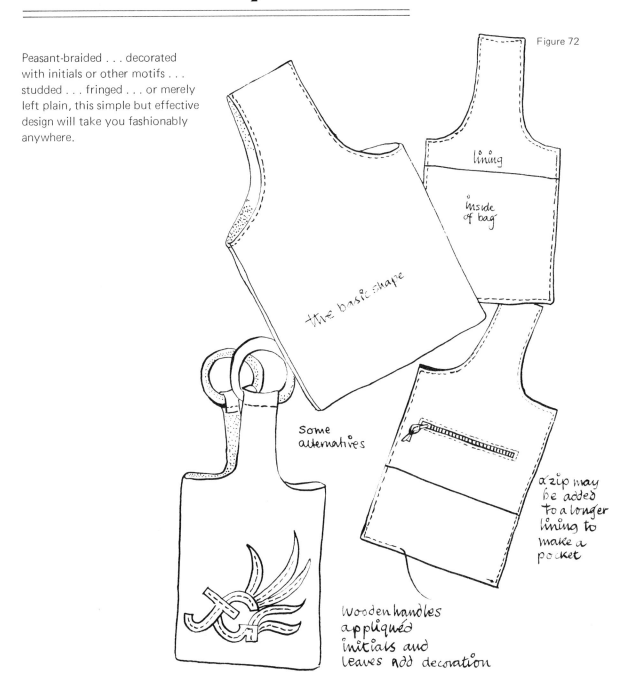

Figure 72

lining

inside
of bag

the basic shape

some
alternatives

a zip may
be added
to a longer
lining to
make a
pocket

Wooden handles
appliquéd
initials and
leaves add decoration

You could, of course, make it in
patchwork, or more spectacularly
in gold or silver kid!

## Pattern preparing

Cut an oblong ABCD from paper as shown in figure 73. Fold in half along H—H. Mark G 18 cm (7 in) down H—C. Repeat on H—D, H—A and H—B. Mark E and F 5 cm (2 in) either side of the centre line.

Fold the pattern at H—H and then fold again as shown in figure 74. At both points H, draw a 45° diagonal line 16 cm (6½ in) long and mark J. Join F—J—F and cut out the curve through the four thicknesses of paper. Then open up the pattern.

## Skin cutting

Cut two bag shapes in leather. Then cut two handle linings following the bag shape down to 5 cm (2 in) below both points G.

Figure 73

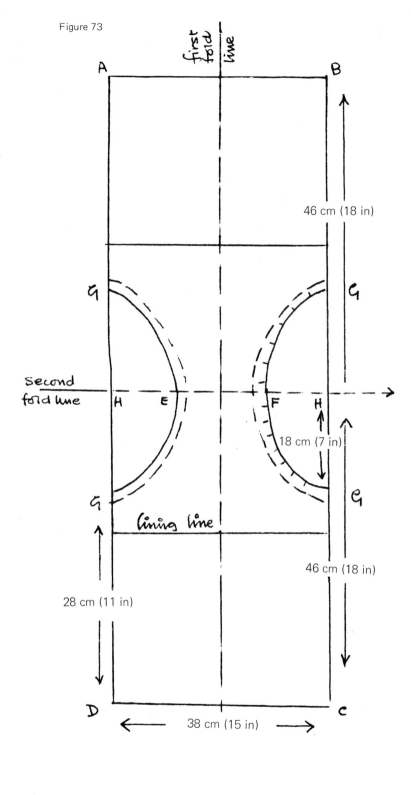

Figure 74

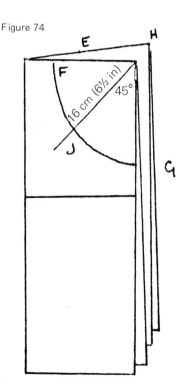

58

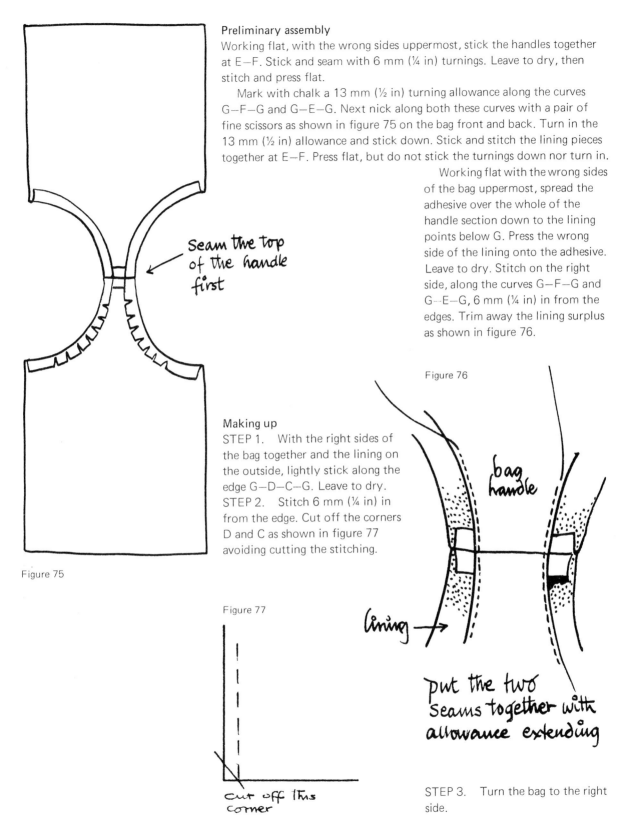

### Preliminary assembly

Working flat, with the wrong sides uppermost, stick the handles together at E—F. Stick and seam with 6 mm (¼ in) turnings. Leave to dry, then stitch and press flat.

Mark with chalk a 13 mm (½ in) turning allowance along the curves G—F—G and G—E—G. Next nick along both these curves with a pair of fine scissors as shown in figure 75 on the bag front and back. Turn in the 13 mm (½ in) allowance and stick down. Stick and stitch the lining pieces together at E—F. Press flat, but do not stick the turnings down nor turn in.

Working flat with the wrong sides of the bag uppermost, spread the adhesive over the whole of the handle section down to the lining points below G. Press the wrong side of the lining onto the adhesive. Leave to dry. Stitch on the right side, along the curves G—F—G and G—E—G, 6 mm (¼ in) in from the edges. Trim away the lining surplus as shown in figure 76.

Seam the top of the handle first

### Making up

STEP 1.   With the right sides of the bag together and the lining on the outside, lightly stick along the edge G—D—C—G. Leave to dry.
STEP 2.   Stitch 6 mm (¼ in) in from the edge. Cut off the corners D and C as shown in figure 77 avoiding cutting the stitching.

Figure 75

Figure 76

bag handle

lining →

put the two seams together with allowance extending

Figure 77

cut off this corner

STEP 3.   Turn the bag to the right side.

# Flower Satchel Set

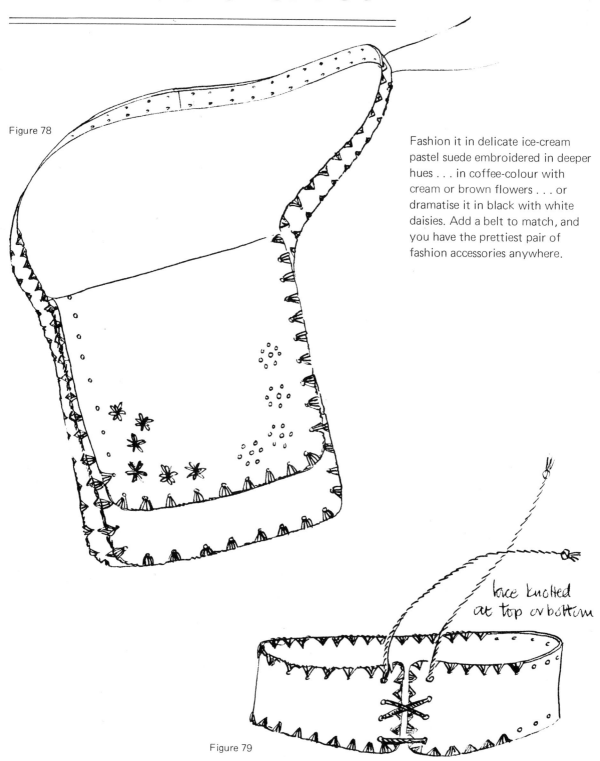

Figure 78

Fashion it in delicate ice-cream pastel suede embroidered in deeper hues . . . in coffee-colour with cream or brown flowers . . . or dramatise it in black with white daisies. Add a belt to match, and you have the prettiest pair of fashion accessories anywhere.

lace knotted at top or bottom

Figure 79

## THE SATCHEL

### Pattern preparing for the bag

For the bag back, cut an oblong 44 x 21 cm (17¼ x 8¼ in). Round off the four corners with a glass tumbler. For the bag front, cut a smaller oblong 20 x 21 cm (8 x 8¼). Round off the two lower corners only with a tumbler. Then mark the gusset/shoulder strap 66 cm x 18 mm (26 x ¾ in).

### Skin cutting

Cut one bag front and one back in suede. Repeat in lining leather or fabric. Then cut two gusset/shoulder straps in leather.

### Preliminary assembly

Punch the holes for the flowers and embroider them in lazy daisy stitch (figure 80) before making up the bag so that the reverse of the stitching is hidden by the lining.

Figure 80

On the wrong side, seam the gusset and seam the shoulder strap top as shown in figure 81. Then stick the ends together, leave to dry and stitch. Press flat and stick down.

With the wrong sides together, stick the lining to the bag back and the front. Leave to dry. Then punch the holes 13 mm (½ in) in from the edge, round the four sides of the back (including the flap-over), about 18 mm (¾ in) from the centre to centre.

Repeat on the sides and the lower edges only of the bag front.

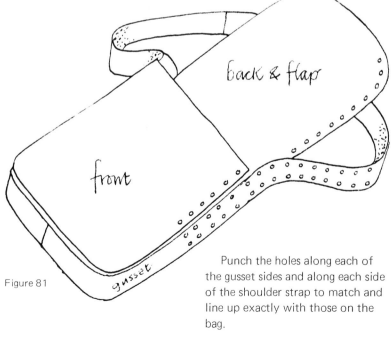

Figure 81

Punch the holes along each of the gusset sides and along each side of the shoulder strap to match and line up exactly with those on the bag.

## Making up

STEP 1.    With the wrong sides together, place one gusset seam centrally as shown in figure 81. Secure one side of the strip to the bottom and the side of the back lower half with paperclips. Stick and leave to dry, then stitch.

STEP 2.    Starting at the same point, stick the other side of the strip to the bag front. Leave to dry and stitch.

STEP 3.    Nick the inside curved corners. Then finish the front opening corners with hand-staystitching.

STEP 4.    Crochet or blanketstitch round all the punch-holed edges with embroidery wool or silk, continuing along both sides of the shoulder strap (figure 82). Then finish off the thread ends neatly.

Figure 82

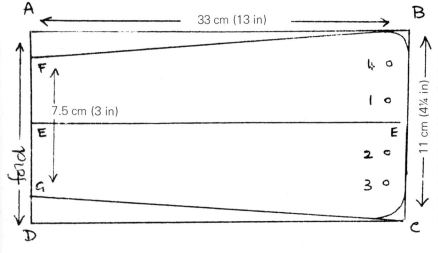

## MATCHING LACE-UP BELT

### Pattern preparing

Cut an oblong 66 x 11 cm (26 x 4¼ in) as in figure 83. Fold in half to make ABCD 33 x 11 cm (13 x 4¼ in). Mark E and E at the centre of A–D and B–C. Join E–E.

Along A–E–D, 4 cm (1½ in) above and below E, mark F and G, in total measuring 7.5 cm (3 in). Join F and G respectively to B and C. Round off the corners B and C.

Then mark lacing holes along B–E–C beginning with 1 and 2 on figure 81, 13 mm (½ in) either side of line E. Then mark 3 and 4 above and below 1 and 2.

### Skin cutting

Cut one belt shape FGCB in suede, and another in lining leather. Depending on how far the lacing is to extend, prepare the thonging according to the instructions given for Puffills on page 84.

Figure 83

*Diagram as for 66cm (26in) waist*

33 cm (13 in)

A    B

F

7.5 cm (3 in)

E    E

G    11 cm (4¼ in)

fold

D    C

## Making up

STEP 1.    With the wrong sides together, stick the lining to the belt. Leave to dry.

STEP 2.    Punch small holes round the top and the bottom edges as for the Satchel.

STEP 3.    Finish off with the same fancy edging stitch. Then lace the eyelets, and bead or fringe the thonging ends.

# Dashing Dollybag

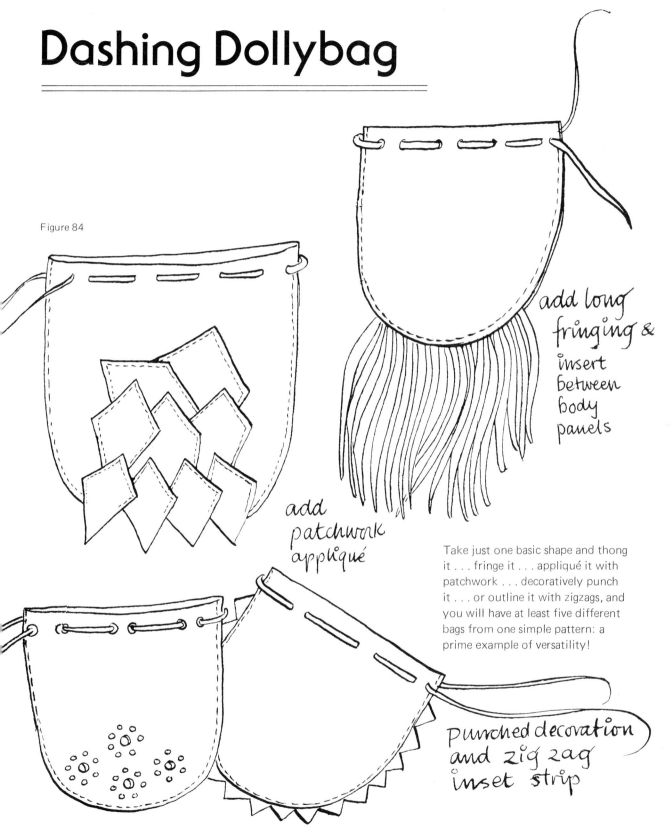

Figure 84

add long fringing & insert between body panels

add patchwork appliqué

Take just one basic shape and thong it . . . fringe it . . . appliqué it with patchwork . . . decoratively punch it . . . or outline it with zigzags, and you will have at least five different bags from one simple pattern: a prime example of versatility!

punched decoration and zig zag inset strip

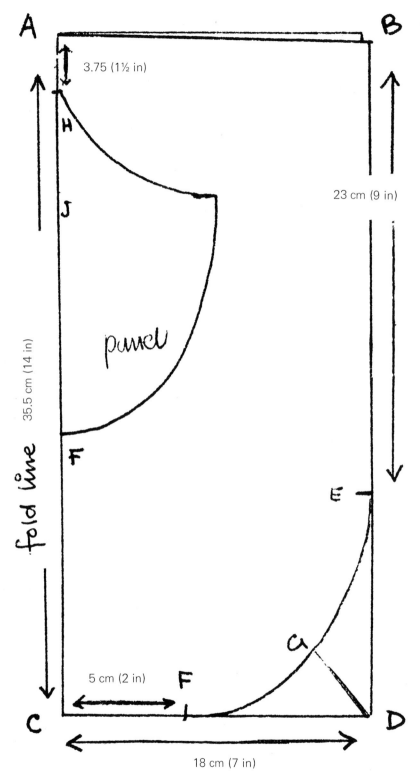

A

B

3.75 (1½ in)

H

23 cm (9 in)

J

panel

35.5 cm (14 in)

fold line

F

E

5 cm (2 in)    F

G

C

F

D

18 cm (7 in)

Figure 85

## THE BASIC DOLLYBAG

### Pattern preparing

Fold a square 35.5 x 35.5 cm (14 x 14 in) in half lengthways to an oblong ABCD 35.5 x 18 cm (14 x 7 in) as shown in figure 85. Mark E 23 cm (9 in) down B—D and F 5 cm (2 in) along C—D. At the corner D make a 45° angle and mark G 6 cm (2½ in) along it. Join the F—G—E curve. Do not include the 'panel' for this basic bag.

### Skin cutting

Cut two bag body shapes in leather, the back 13 mm (½ in) larger than the front to facilitate machining nearer to the edge. Cut, or buy, 6 mm (¼ in) thonging. Cut a draw-string strip 3 x 212 cm ($1\frac{1}{8}$ x 84 in). Fold and stitch as shown in figure 30, and make a loop (figure 31).

### Preliminary assembly

Open out the pattern. Mark eyelet holes on both sides of the bag as shown in figure 86 with eyelet 1 19 mm (¾ in) from the centre, and eyelets 2, 3 and 4 at 3.75 cm (1½ in) from each other. Repeat for the other side, leaving the top opening edge raw.

### Making up

STEP 1.   Place the two body shapes with the wrong sides together, and stick the front edges centrally on the back, but with the top edges lined up.

STEP 2.   Machine, as close to the edge as possible, round C—F—G—E—B. Trim away the 13 mm (½ in) surplus from the back.

STEP 3.   Punch smaller holes 13 mm (½ in) in from the edge along B—C—B of both bag shapes, 2.5 cm (1 in) centre to centre. Overlace with thonging, then tuck in the ends neatly (figure 87).

STEP 4.   Thread the drawstring through the eyelet holes and fringe or knot the ends.

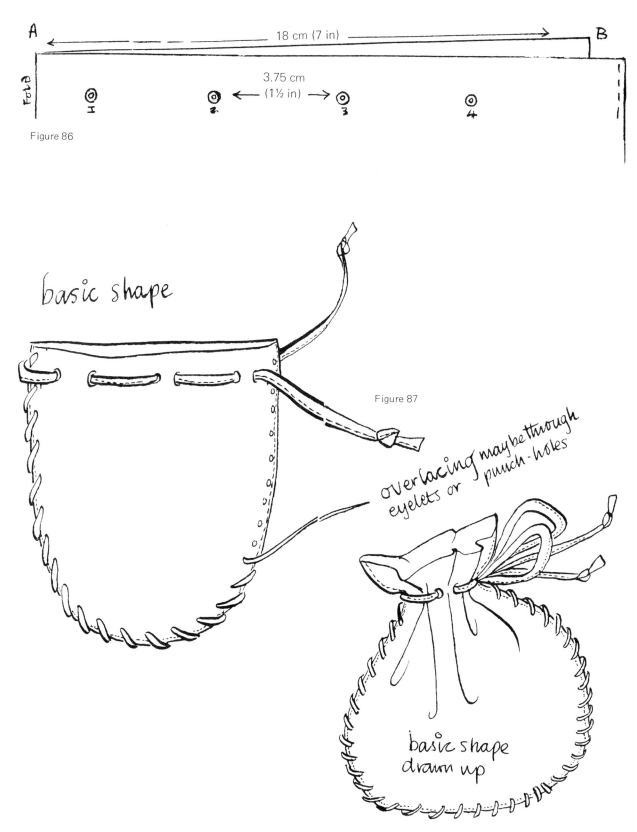

A

18 cm (7 in)

B

Fold

3.75 cm
(1½ in)

1

2

3

4

Figure 86

basic shape

Figure 87

overlacing may be through
eyelets or punch-holes

basic shape
drawn up

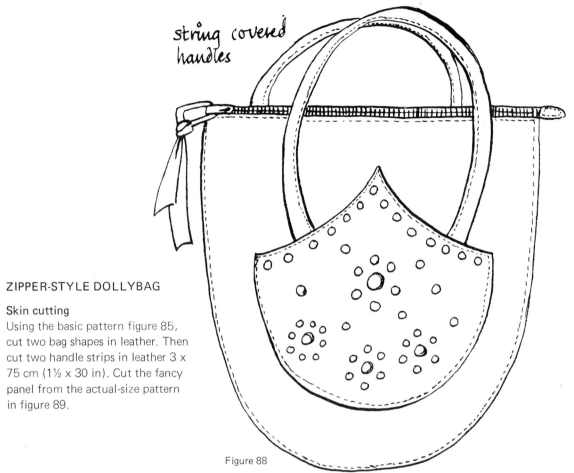

string covered handles

Figure 88

decorative punched panel covers ends of stitched and folded handles.

## ZIPPER-STYLE DOLLYBAG

### Skin cutting

Using the basic pattern figure 85, cut two bag shapes in leather. Then cut two handle strips in leather 3 x 75 cm (1½ x 30 in). Cut the fancy panel from the actual-size pattern in figure 89.

### Preliminary assembly

Decorate the panel first. On the bag front, mark H 3 cm (1½ in) directly below A on the fold, and F 14 cm (5½ in) directly below H. Then mark L on the panel.

Make up the handles as shown in the directions in figure 32. Leave to dry. Then stick each handle under the edges of the panel at L and L as shown in figure 88. Then working flat, lay the bag shapes face downwards, and insert the zip following the instructions on page 23.

Turn the bag over, but still working flat, place the wrong side of the panel to the right side of the bag front, and match the points already marked. Stick along the lower curve of the panel only. Place it under a weight to set. Before stitching the edges, make sure at least 2.5 cm (1 in) of the handle ends are firmly inside before stitching across them.

Mark two 13 mm (½ in) slits for the handles on the bag back, 10 cm (4 in) down from the top edge, and 13 mm (½ in) below the point on the back corresponding.

On the right side of the bag back, insert the handle ends through the slits. Cover the ends with small squares of leather and stick down both of the layers to the inside of the bag. Leave to set under a heavy weight. Finally, on the right side, stitch twice across the slits.

Figure 89

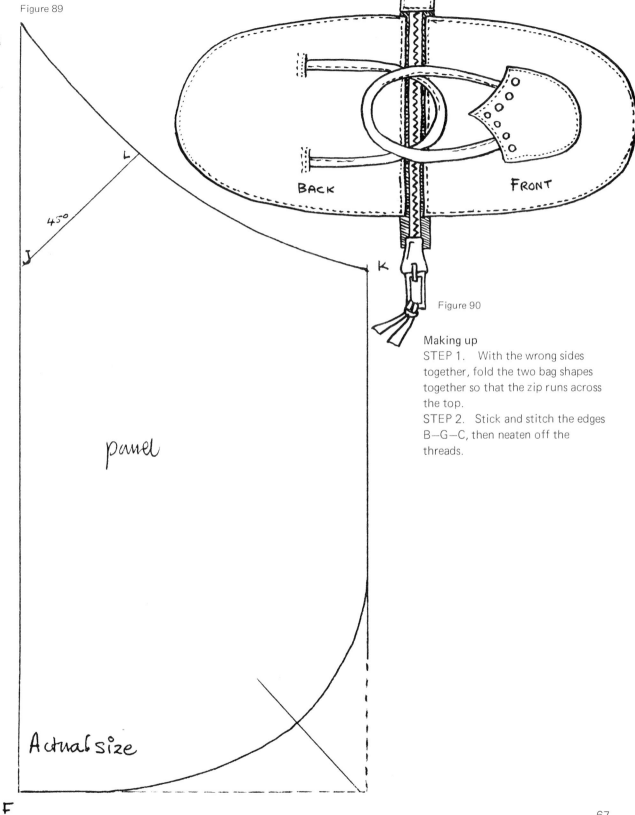

H

L

45°

J

K

panel

Actual size

F

BACK

FRONT

Figure 90

## Making up
STEP 1.　With the wrong sides together, fold the two bag shapes together so that the zip runs across the top.
STEP 2.　Stick and stitch the edges B—G—C, then neaten off the threads.

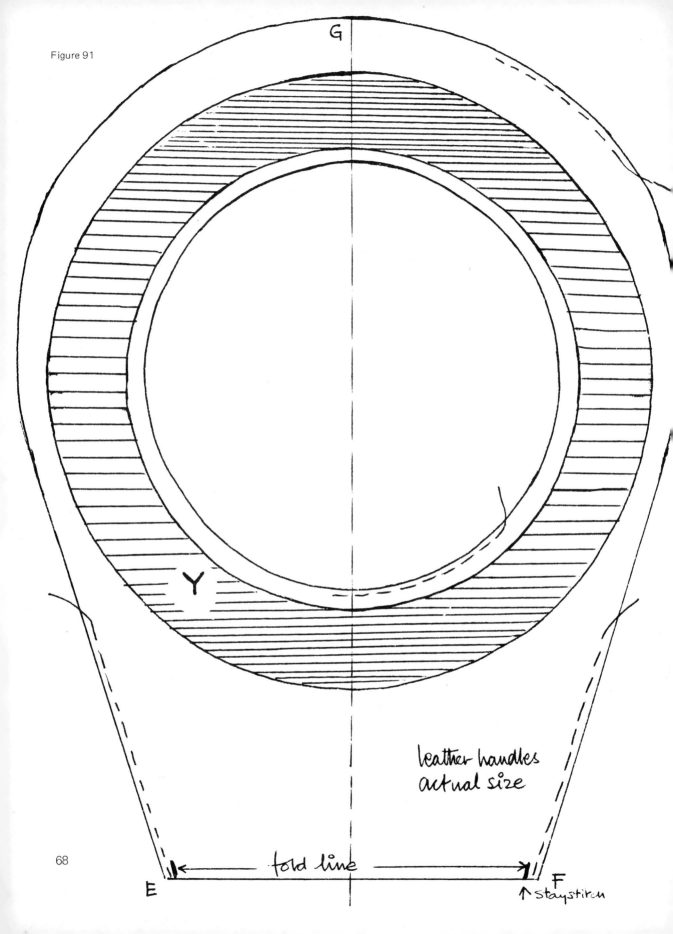

Figure 91

G

Y

leather handles
actual size

E    fold line    F

68    ↑ staystitch

## DOLLYBAG WITH SHAPED HANDLES

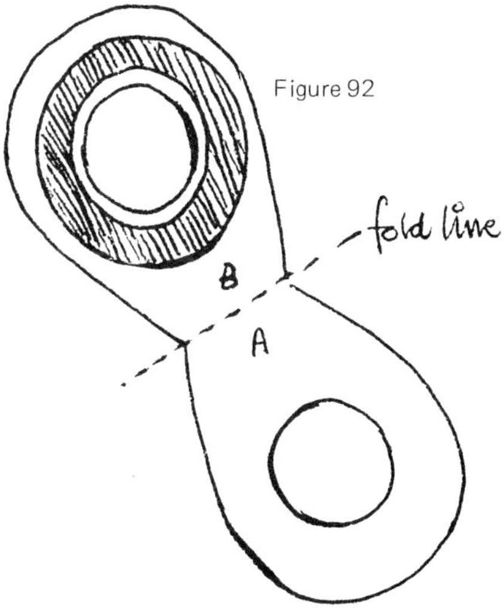

### Pattern preparing
For the bag, follow the basic pattern in figure 85. Cut the handle pattern from the actual-size pattern in figure 91.

### Skin cutting
Cut two bag shapes in leather. Then cut two handle shapes in leather. Cut two reinforcing cardboard rings as shown on the shaded area Y on figure 91.

### Preliminary assembly
Mark the eyelet holes on the bag as for the basic design. Open out each handle from the fold line. On the wrong side, stick the cardboard circle round one centre circle as shown in figure 92. Repeat for the other handle, and leave both to dry.

With the right sides together, lay the opened-out centre fold line of the handle centrally 2.5 cm (1 in) below the eyelets as shown in figure 93. Stitch firmly with a double row of stitching along the fold line on the wrong side of the handle. Knot these ends off firmly. Repeat for the other handle.

Spread adhesive over the wrong side of the complete handle section B, including the cardboard ring. Press the wrong side of A to it as shown in figure 94. Anchor together with paperclips and leave to dry. Stitch the inner ring as near to the edge as possible. Repeat on the other handle.

Fold back the top of the bag to avoid stitching through the bag body. Stitch round the outer edge of the handle EGF. Now press the folded edge EP flat to the body of the bag so that the inner stitching is hidden.

Stabstitch firmly by hand at the corners A and F right through both sections of the handle plus the bag body. Stitch by hand along the outside of this fold. Repeat for the other handle.

Figure 92

fold line

B

A

Figure 93

B

A

front

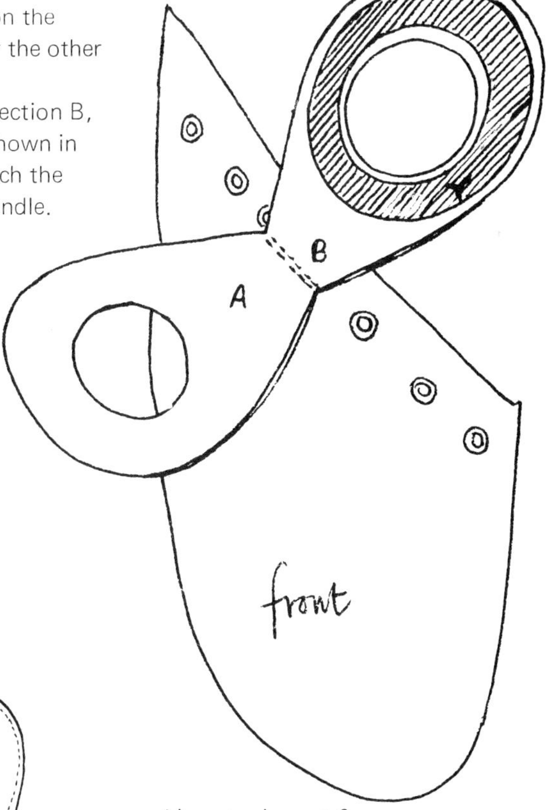

Figure 94

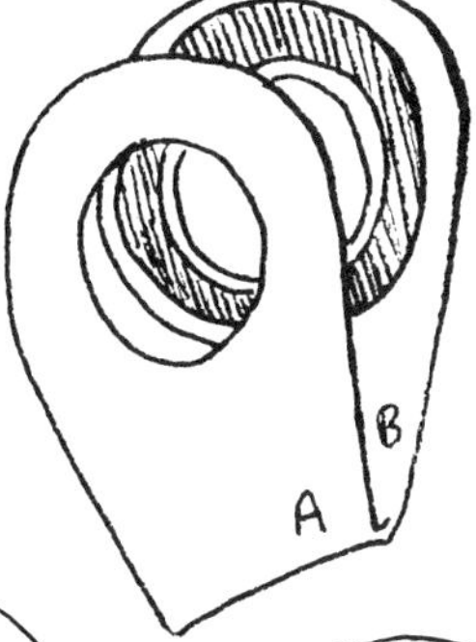

B

A

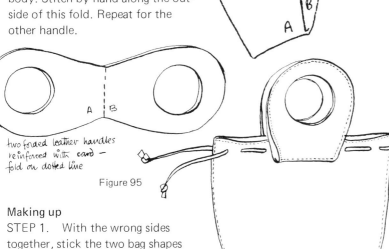

two folded leather handles reinforced with card — fold on dotted line

A | B

Figure 95

attach handle to front of bag — repeat for back

### Making up
STEP 1. With the wrong sides together, stick the two bag shapes together. Leave to dry, and stitch.

STEP 2. Stick a 13 mm (½ in) tape above the eyelet holes inside the bag top if the leather seems to be too stretchy.

# Take a Pear Shape...

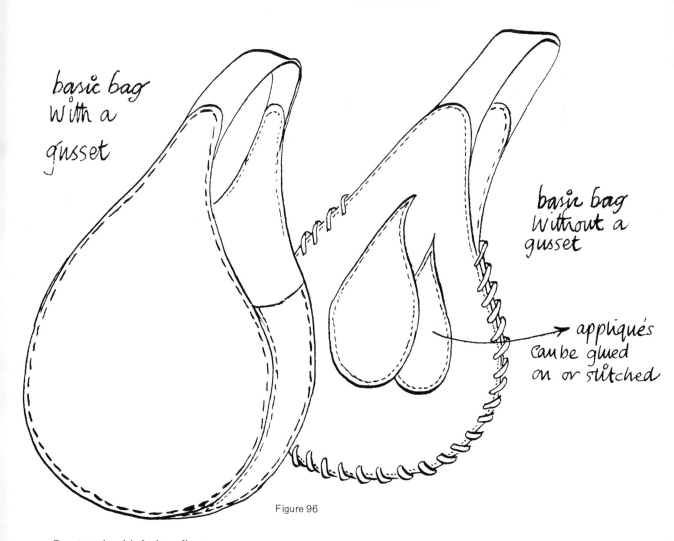

basic bag
with a
gusset

basic bag
without a
gusset

appliqués
can be glued
on or stitched

Figure 96

Decorate it with fruit or flower
motifs . . . punch patterns on it . . .
or add stick-on beads; from one
attractively curved basic shape you
can create endless and striking
variations.

# THE BASIC PEAR-SHAPE BAG

## Pattern preparing

Mark the bag shape using the pattern on the end papers at the back of the book. Mark one lining shape down as far as H—J on the bag. Then mark an oblong 12 x 5 cm (5 x 2 in) for the handle.

## Skin cutting

Cut two bag shapes in leather. Then cut two lining shapes, also in leather. Cut two oblongs for the handles. Finally cut the thonging as given in Puffills on page 84.

## Preliminary assembly

Apply any motifs first to the bag front. With the wrong sides together, stick one handle oblong on top of the other. Sandwich the oblong end between the lining as shown in figure 97 and the bag body at K, and fasten together with paperclips, seeing that K and K are 5 cm (2 in) apart as shown on the pattern.

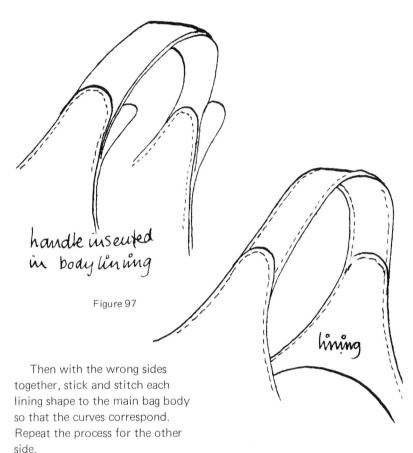

handle inserted in body lining

Figure 97

lining

Then with the wrong sides together, stick and stitch each lining shape to the main bag body so that the curves correspond. Repeat the process for the other side.

## Making up

STEP 1.  With the wrong sides together, take the two bag bodies and match the points H and J.

STEP 2.  Stick and stitch on the right side from A—X—B, taking care that the handle lining points H and J lie below the stitching ends at A and B. Hand-staystitch at these points.

STEP 3.  Punch and overlace along A—X—B.

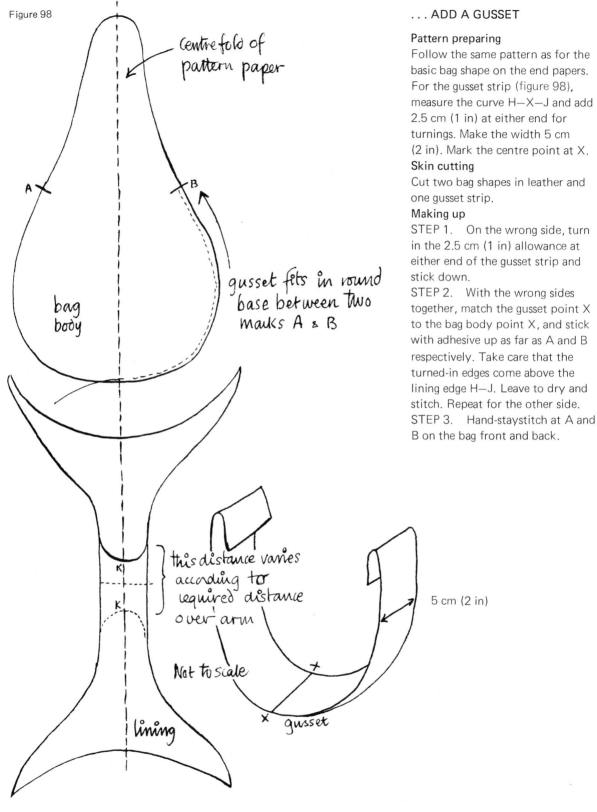

Figure 98

centre fold of pattern paper

A

B

bag body

gusset fits in round base between two marks A & B

this distance varies according to required distance over arm

K

K

Not to scale

lining

5 cm (2 in)

x gusset

## ... ADD A GUSSET

### Pattern preparing
Follow the same pattern as for the basic bag shape on the end papers. For the gusset strip (figure 98), measure the curve H—X—J and add 2.5 cm (1 in) at either end for turnings. Make the width 5 cm (2 in). Mark the centre point at X.

### Skin cutting
Cut two bag shapes in leather and one gusset strip.

### Making up
STEP 1.   On the wrong side, turn in the 2.5 cm (1 in) allowance at either end of the gusset strip and stick down.

STEP 2.   With the wrong sides together, match the gusset point X to the bag body point X, and stick with adhesive up as far as A and B respectively. Take care that the turned-in edges come above the lining edge H—J. Leave to dry and stitch. Repeat for the other side.

STEP 3.   Hand-staystitch at A and B on the bag front and back.

# Trendy
# Nosebag

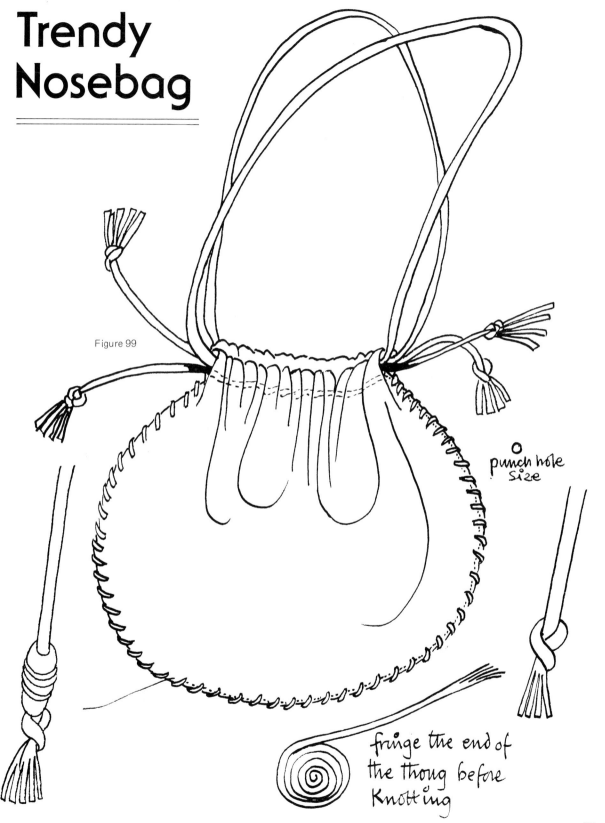

Figure 99

O punch hole
size

fringe the end of
the thong before
knotting

Softly pleated, in key with the unstructured lines of fashion, this up-to-the-minute bag leaves your hands free for shopping or coping with children.

It lends itself to all kinds of decoration, but it looks equally good unadorned.

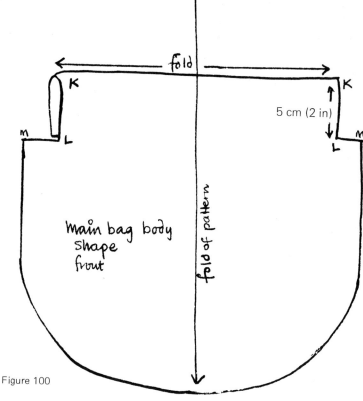

Figure 100

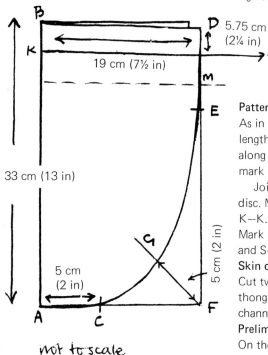

not to scale

## Pattern preparing

As in figure 100, mark an oblong 33 x 38 cm (13 x 15 in) and fold in half lengthways to form ABDF 33 x 19 cm (13 x 7½ in). Mark C 5 cm (2 in) along A—F, and E 14 cm (8 in) directly below D. With a 45° angle from F, mark G 5.75 cm (2¼ in) along it.

Join the A—C—G—E—D curve, drawing round an LP or similar-sized disc. Mark K—K 5 cm (2 in) below B—D, and M—M 5 cm (2 in) below K—K. On M—M mark L and L 3 cm (1½ in) in from M and M (figure 101). Mark P 3 cm (1½ in) in from D, and S 3 cm (1½ in) in from B. Join P—L and S—L. Cut PLM and SLM.

## Skin cutting

Cut two bag shapes in leather. Then cut two lengths of 180 cm (72 in) thonging. Cut a 50 cm (20 in) length of 13 mm (½ in) elastic. For the channel tube, cut a strip 3 x 45 cm (1½ x 19 in) in leather.

## Preliminary assembly

On the bag front, pleat M under L as shown in figure 103 so that the wrong side looks like figure 104. Stick firmly, and lightly stitch on the back of the pleat so that the stitching does not show through. Repeat on the other corner.

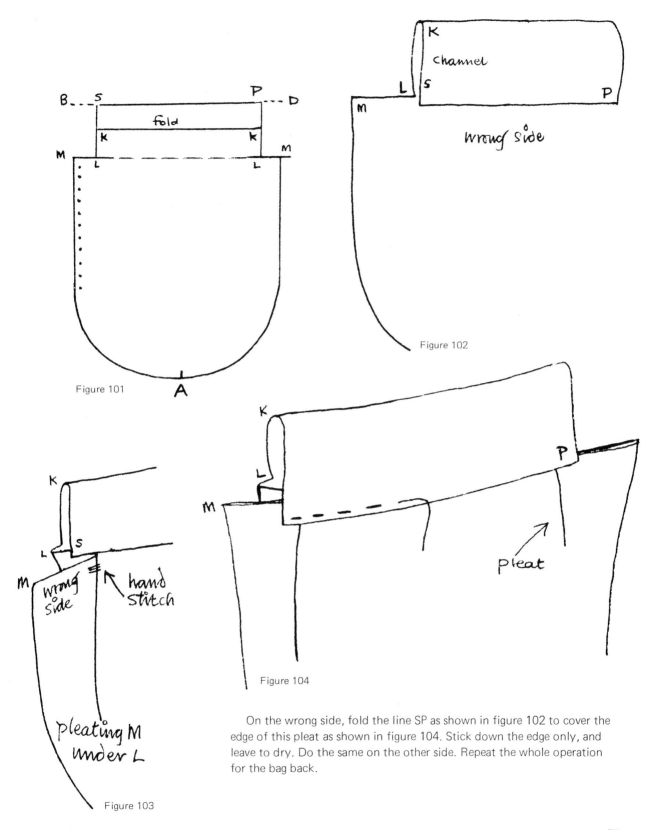

B ....  S                                P  .... D

fold

K                                K

M                                M
L                                L

A

Figure 101

K

channel

L  S

M

P

wrong side

Figure 102

K

L

M  wrong
side

S

hand
stitch

pleating M
under L

Figure 103

K

L

M

P

pleat

Figure 104

On the wrong side, fold the line SP as shown in figure 102 to cover the edge of this pleat as shown in figure 104. Stick down the edge only, and leave to dry. Do the same on the other side. Repeat the whole operation for the bag back.

## Making up

STEP 1.    On the wrong side, double stitch along L—L on the bag front and back. With the wrong sides of the two body sections together, stick and stitch along L/M—A—L/M. Leave to dry. Make punch holes along the M—A—M curve. Overlace.

STEP 2.    Make the channel tube by folding the strip in half lengthways, then stitching the sides together as shown in figure 105. Thread the elastic through the tube leaving both ends exposed, then hold together with paper-clips.

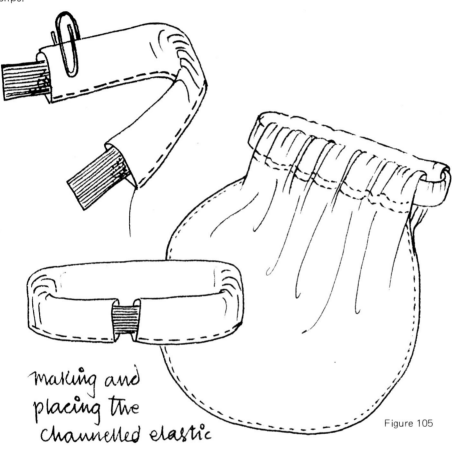

making and placing the channelled elastic

Figure 105

STEP 3.    Thread the covered elastic through the folded top of the bag back and front, and pull the elastic out at one side. Stitch both ends of the elastic together. Ease the elastic round to the back of the fold so that only the leather is visible on either side.

STEP 4.    Take one length of the neck thonging and insert it left to right through the gathered top of the bag back. Thread through the other end in reverse. Finish off the ends with a bead and a knot. Repeat for the other bag section.

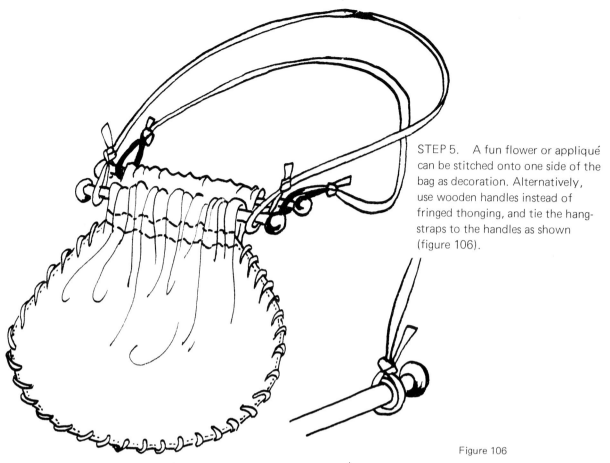

STEP 5.   A fun flower or appliqué can be stitched onto one side of the bag as decoration. Alternatively, use wooden handles instead of fringed thonging, and tie the hang-straps to the handles as shown (figure 106).

Figure 106

variations on a pattern theme

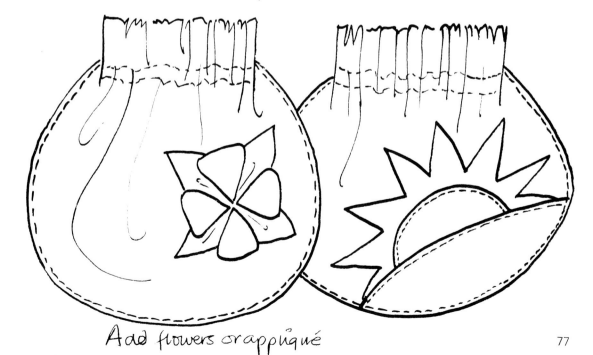

Add flowers or appliqué

# Cool Clutch

Easily converted from an elegant classic to a sturdy workaday type of clutch. It can be thonged . . . peasant-braided . . . or striped with contrast-coloured leather or suede.

Figure 107

Or if you are feeling thoroughly daring, who not try gold or white thonging on a plain black bag?

### Pattern preparing

Cut an oblong ABCD 28 x 58.5 cm (11 x 23 in) as shown in figure 108. Mark within it a 13 mm (½ in) allowance all the way round. Working on the inner oblong, mark E—M 16.5 cm (6½ in) above D—C.

Then mark F—G 19 mm (¾ in) above E—M. This forms the bag base EMGF. Mark J—H 16.5 cm (6½ in) above F—G. Then mark K—L halfway between A—J and B—H. Then cut round ABCD.

For the gusset, cut another oblong CHMG 18 x 7 cm (7½ x 3 in). Round off the corners M and G as shown in figure 109. Inside, mark a 13 mm (½ in) turning all the way round. For the flap stiffener, cut an oblong 22 x 8 cm (9 x 3½ in).

### Cutting the skin

Cut one bag shape in leather, and another in lining leather. Then cut two gussets in leather. In thicker *side* leather, cut one flap stiffener.

### Preliminary assembly

Cut off diagonally the main corners A, B, C and D. Make a V-shaped nick as shown in J and H in figure 108. Turn in the three edges J—A—B—H so that the corners A and B are mitred as shown in figure 110. Then stick the flap stiffener within this inner oblong.

Turn the work over and place it, face downwards, onto the wrong side of the lining as shown in figure 111. Stick over the complete area as far as J and H. Leave to dry. On the right side, stitch round the sides J—A—B—H. Then dart the gusset tops as shown in figure 109.

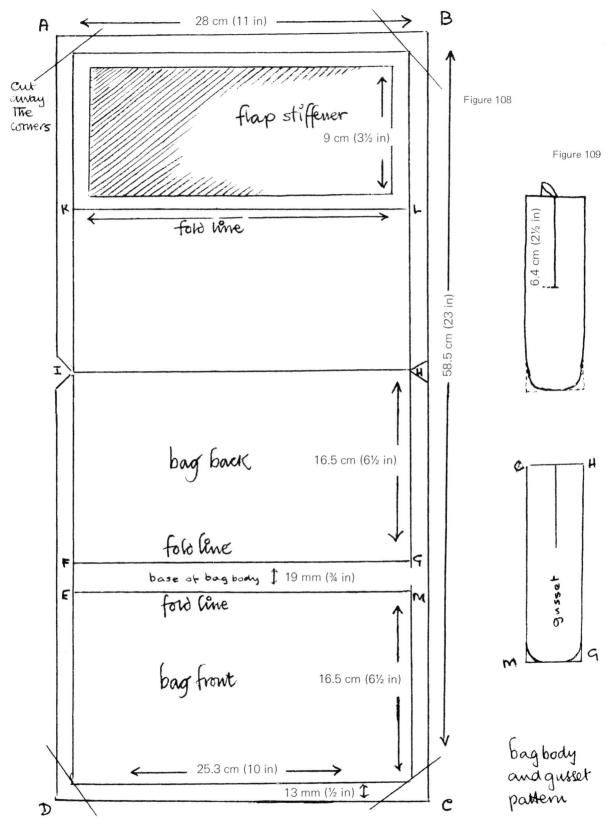

A — 28 cm (11 in) — B

Cut away the corners

flap stiffener

9 cm (3½ in)

K — fold line — L

Figure 108

Figure 109

6.4 cm (2½ in)

58.5 cm (23 in)

I — H

bag back

16.5 cm (6½ in)

fold line

F — G

base of bag body  ↕ 19 mm (¾ in)

E — M

fold line

bag front

16.5 cm (6½ in)

G — H

gusset

M — G

25.3 cm (10 in)

13 mm (½ in) ↕

D — C

bag body and gusset pattern

79

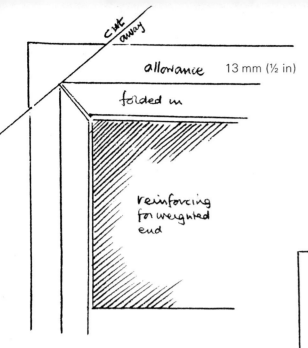

cut away

allowance 13 mm (½ in)

folded in

reinforcing for weighted end

Figure 110

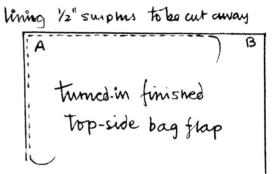

lining ½" surplus to be cut away

A

B

turned-in finished Top-side bag flap

Figure 111

Figure 112

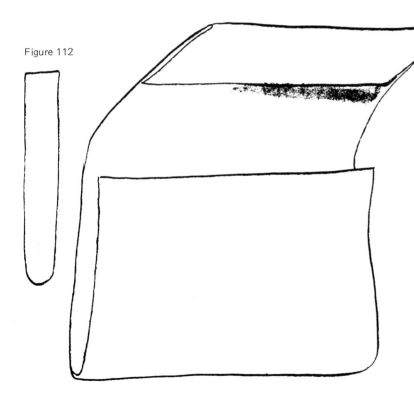

**Making up**

STEP 1.   On the main bag, turn in the 13 mm (½ in) allowance D—C. With the right sides together, place the gusset point C to the bag point C. Match the Ms and Gs, easing round the gusset curve. Continue up the bag back and match H to H. Stick, leave to dry and stitch. For the other gusset, match D to C, E to M, F to G and J to H. Then hand-staystitch at the corners to strengthen them.

STEP 2.   Turn the bag inside out and make small nicks along the gusset curves. Working on the flat, turn the bag to the right side with the wrong side of the flap towards you. Hold the loose lining with the right hand and spread the adhesive

inside the back of the bag downwards from J and H. Press the
wrong side of the lining inside the
bag to the wrong side of the back.
STEP 3.    Spread the adhesive
along the base FGEM and press the
lining onto it.
STEP 4.    Turn the work over onto
the front and spread the adhesive
over the inside of the bag front.
Press the wrong side of the lining
inside the bag to the wrong side of
the bag front. Stick the lining
surplus so that it covers the inside
gusset seams. Neaten the D—C edge
and the lining. Trim off all the
surplus lining.
STEP 5.    This bag can be
decorated by punching holes round
the edges and overlacing as shown
(figure 113). Alternatively, the bag
can be squared up to form a purse
shape (figure 114).

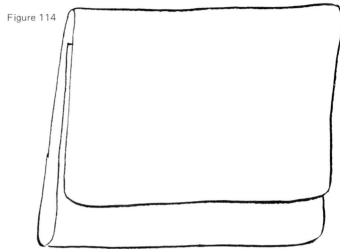

oblong underarm clutchbag
or squared up if
required as a purse

Figure 114

weighted end holds-flat
without
fastening

Figure 113

using same pattern and
with outside seams
punched and overlaced

# Puffills

Hang these attractive soft leather puffy baglets in pairs, or clusters, round your neck, or girdling your waist or hips.

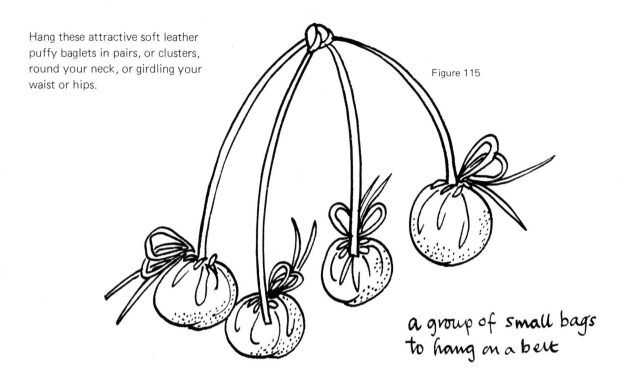

Figure 115

*a group of small bags to hang on a belt*

Perhaps you prefer them in contrasting colours . . . in patchwork . . . or more ethnically in natural colour leathers?

Whether you want them for daytime or after-six socialising, though, they are the swingiest fashion accessories about town.

### Making the pattern
Fold the paper in half and trace figure 116 off the page, which is a half pattern. Cut it out, open out the paper, and mark on the letters as given in figure 117.

### Cutting the skin
Cut one circle shape in leather from the pattern. On another piece of leather mark, on the wrong side, a 13 mm (1 in) wide facing rim using the outer and inner circle lines as a guide. Then cut out.

The remainder of the rim circle can be used to cut out a 6 mm (¼ in) drawstring thong as shown in figure 118, starting from the outside and working inwards. Cut and make a hangstrap as in Miss Moneybags on page 38.

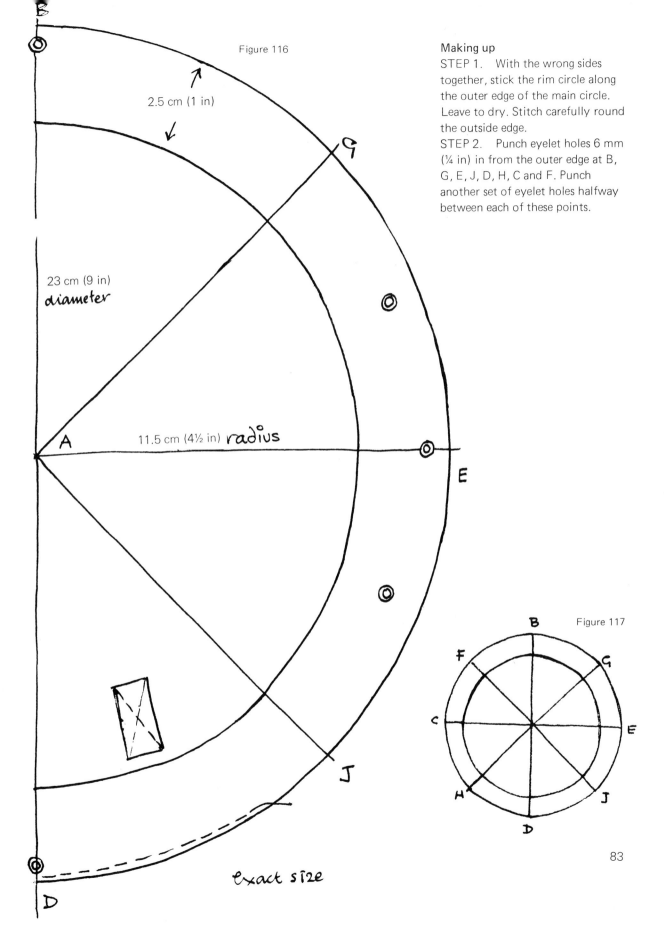

B

Figure 116

2.5 cm (1 in)

G

23 cm (9 in)
diameter

A          11.5 cm (4½ in) radius

E

J

exact size

D

**Making up**

STEP 1.   With the wrong sides together, stick the rim circle along the outer edge of the main circle. Leave to dry. Stitch carefully round the outside edge.

STEP 2.   Punch eyelet holes 6 mm (¼ in) in from the outer edge at B, G, E, J, D, H, C and F. Punch another set of eyelet holes halfway between each of these points.

Figure 117

B
F          G
C                    E
H          J
D

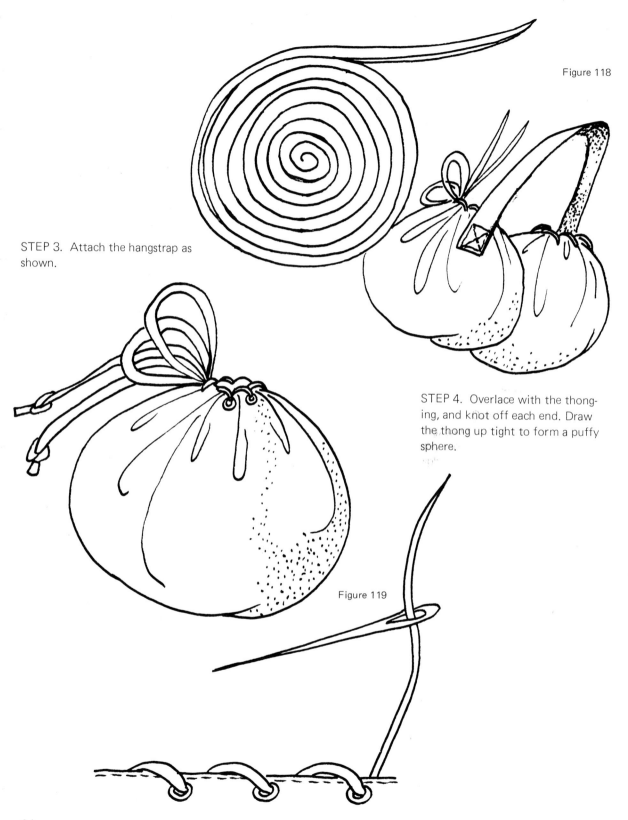

Figure 118

STEP 3. Attach the hangstrap as shown.

STEP 4. Overlace with the thonging, and knot off each end. Draw the thong up tight to form a puffy sphere.

Figure 119

# Touch
# Wood

Figure 120

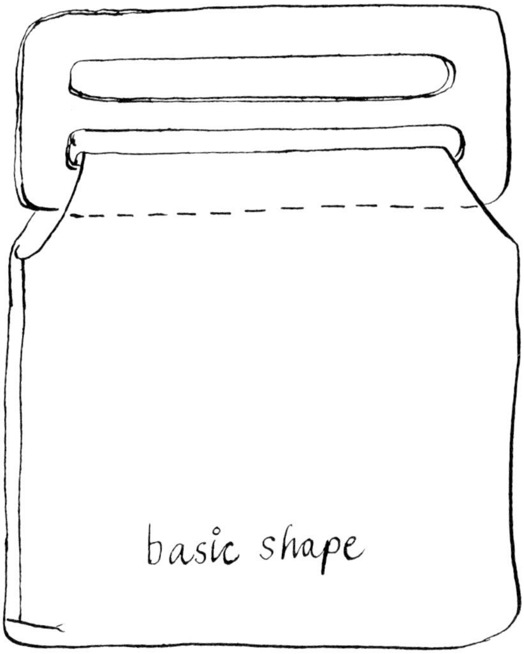

basic shape

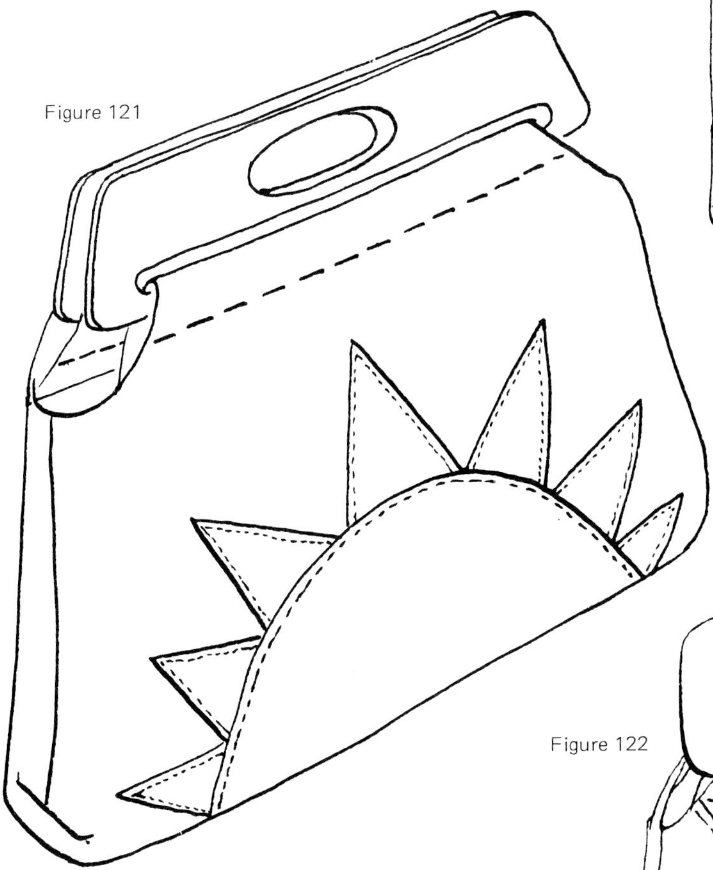

From one basic shape comes a
variety of looks. Add a flower
maybe . . . a fringe . . . decorate it
with bold appliqué motifs . . . or
make it in fancy patchwork, and
you will end up with a bag that will
see you fashionably through the
whole spectrum of socialising.

Figure 121

Figure 122

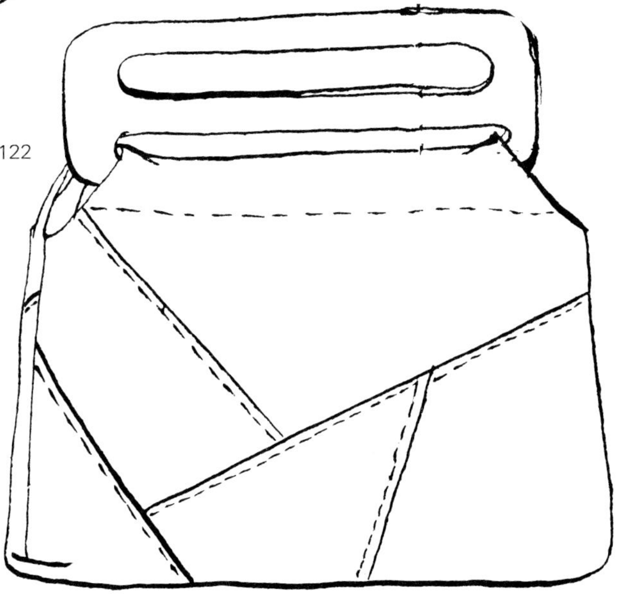

## The handles

Wooden handles in a choice of fancy shapes can be obtained from any good craft shop. Alternatively, anyone skilled in working with wood can easily make some. The ones used in this design have a 26 cm (10½ in) internal slot, and measure 31 cm (12½ in) externally.

Paint them in toning or bold contrasting colours. Or they can look just as attractive coated with wood sealant to bring up the grain.

If you should decide to use colour as a contrast, for extra effectiveness match it to the sewing thread which is used for the stitching that shows.

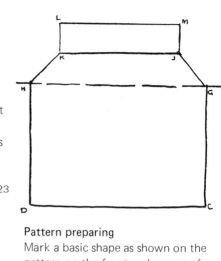

Figure 123

## Pattern preparing

Mark a basic shape as shown on the pattern on the front end papers of this book. Cut round, then open out the pattern on the fold D–C.

## Cutting the skin

Cut one bag shape in leather.

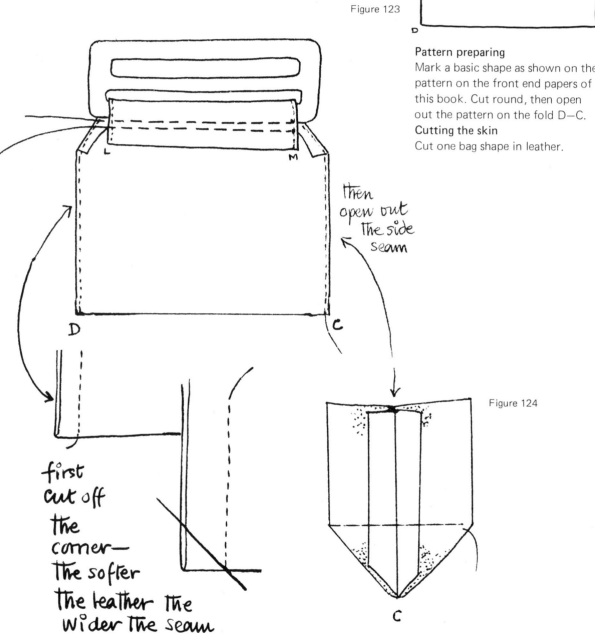

then open out the side seam

first cut off the corner— the softer the leather the wider the seam

Figure 124

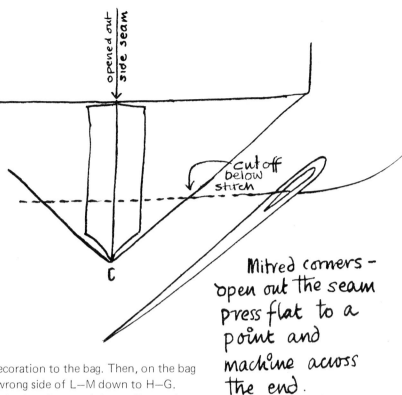

opened out side seam

cut off below stitch

C

Mitred corners – open out the seam press flat to a point and machine across the end.

Figure 125

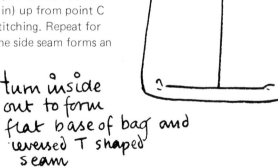

turn inside out to form flat base of bag and reversed T shaped seam

## Making up

STEP 1.    First apply any motif or decoration to the bag. Then, on the bag front, following figure 123, fold the wrong side of L—M down to H—G. Anchor the ends together with paperclips but do not stick yet. Repeat for the bag back.

STEP 2.    With the right sides together, fold the bag body at D—C. Again with the right sides together, stick and stitch the two sides H—D and G—C with 13 mm (½ in) seams.

STEP 3.    Turn the bag inside out. Then mitre the corners by cutting off the corners D and C as shown in figure 124. Next turn one inside seam towards you. Open it out and flatten the seam into a point. Stick down the seam and leave to dry. Stitch across it 13 mm (½ in) up from point C as shown. Cut off the point 6 mm (¼ in) below the stitching. Repeat for the other side. Then turn the bag inside out so that the side seam forms an inverted T-shape as shown in figure 125.

STEP 4.    Make 6 mm (¼ in) horizontal nicks at H and G. Then turn in 13 mm (½ in) along the sides H—K and J—G on the bag back and front. Stick down, leave to dry and stitch.

STEP 5.    With the right side out, measure the handle slot length. Adjust the L—M width accordingly. Then with the wrong sides together, slide L—M through the handle slot and fold back onto the inside of the bag. Stick down at the lower edge L—M. Fasten with paperclips and leave to dry. Then stitch with a double row below the handle as shown. Repeat on the other side.

# Kingsize Bag

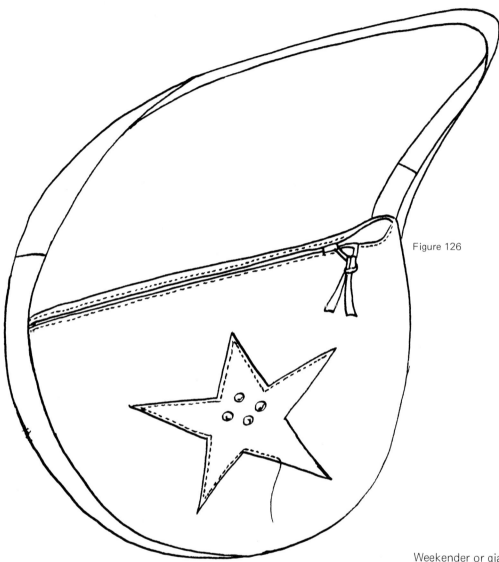

Figure 126

Very large squashy bag

Weekender or giant beachbag, this kingsize container is ideal for carrying swimming paraphernalia . . . a baby's multi-essentials . . . hobby or sports gear . . . or a survival kit.

It is best made in washable leather and, once you have finished it, you will wonder how you ever lived without it!

## Pattern preparing

It is more than likely you will need more than one skin for this design, unless you have a particularly flawless one. Cut a bag shape double the size of the pattern ABGC on the end papers at the back of the book. Mark an oblong 70 x 7.7 cm (28¼ x 3 in) for the gusset. Mark another oblong 100 x 7.7 cm (40 x 3 in) for the shoulder strap, and another 125 x 7.7 cm (50 x 3 in) for its lining. Then mark a further oblong 125 x 5 cm (50 x 2 in) for its canvas interlining

## Skin cutting

Open out the pattern on the fold line A—C and cut two bag shapes in leather. Cut one gusset strip in leather. Cut one shoulder strap in leather, one lining strip, and one canvas interlining strip.

## Preliminary assembly

Decorate the bag first. Then for the assembly of the shoulder strap, stick the canvas interlining centrally to the inside of the lining as shown in figure 128. Leave to dry. On the wrong side, turn in 6 mm (¼ in) along the long sides of the lining to meet the canvas. The width should now measure 6.5 cm (2½ in). Lay aside to dry.

Figure 127

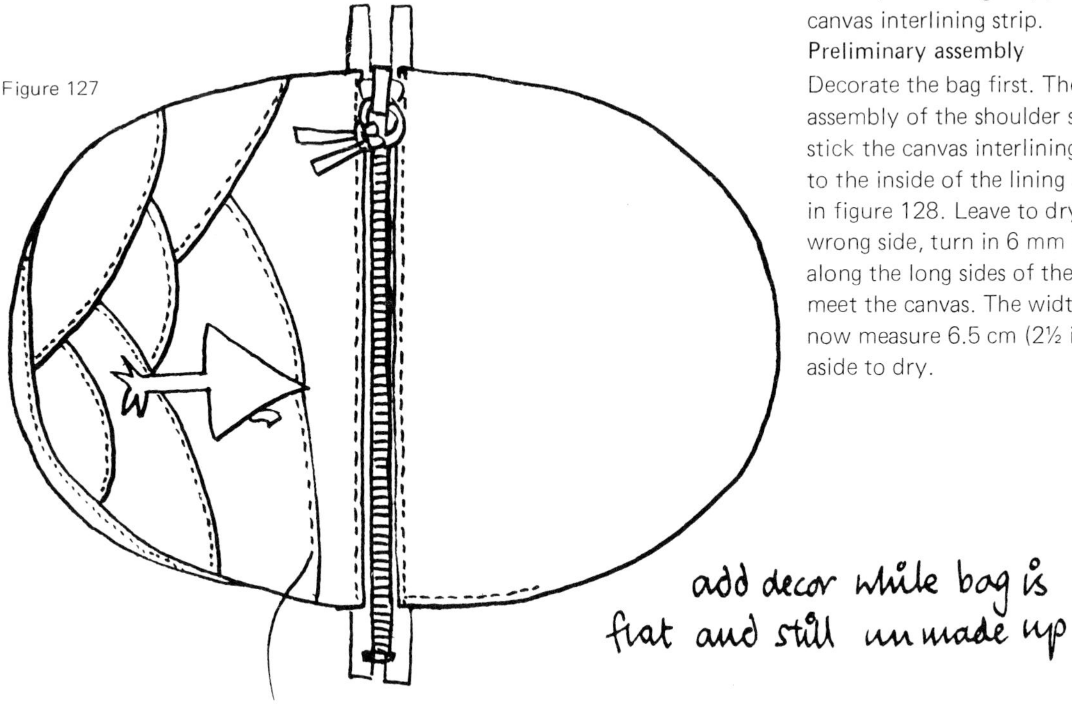

add decor while bag is flat and still un made up

## Making up

STEP 1.   Working flat with the right side uppermost, insert the zip as shown in the instructions on page 23.

STEP 2.   With the right sides together, attach one side of the gusset strip round the side and bottom edges of the bag front using paperclips, leaving a 5 cm (2 in) extension on either side of the zip opening. Stick and leave to dry. Nick the inside curved seams, then stitch. Next attach the other side of the gusset to the bag back and repeat the sewing process. Press the seams flat.

Figure 128

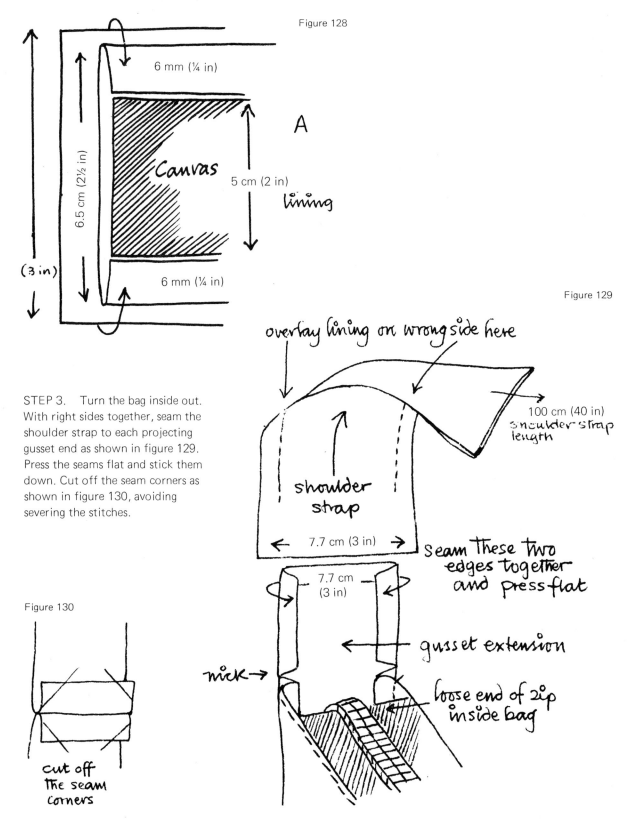

6 mm (¼ in)

A

6.5 cm (2½ in)

Canvas

5 cm (2 in)
lining

(3 in)

6 mm (¼ in)

Figure 129

overlay lining on wrong side here

100 cm (40 in)
shoulder strap
length

shoulder
strap

7.7 cm (3 in)

STEP 3.   Turn the bag inside out.
With right sides together, seam the
shoulder strap to each projecting
gusset end as shown in figure 129.
Press the seams flat and stick them
down. Cut off the seam corners as
shown in figure 130, avoiding
severing the stitches.

seam these two
edges together
and press flat

7.7 cm
(3 in)

gusset extension

nick→

loose end of zip
inside bag

Figure 130

cut off
the seam
corners

90

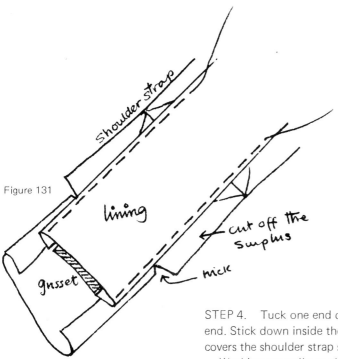

Figure 131

shoulder strap

lining

gusset

cut off the surplus

nick

STEP 4.   Tuck one end of the lining strip inside the bag at the zip stop end. Stick down inside the bag as well as to the gusset extension, so that it covers the shoulder strap seam as shown in figure 131.

   Working centrally so there is a 6 mm (¼ in) surplus of shoulder strap underneath the lining, stick the lining along the shoulder strap to the other end. Taking the other end of the lining, stick it down over the gusset extension as before and to at least 2.5 cm (1 in) inside the bag at the zip end.
STEP 5.   With the shoulder strap lining uppermost, stitch along the edges as far into the bag as the machine will reach. Finish off the ends firmly. Stick down the lining ends firmly covering the gusset top end. Do not stitch across. Trim off the surplus of the shoulder strap as shown in figure 131.

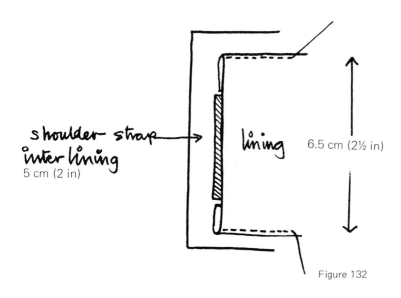

shoulder strap
inter lining
5 cm (2 in)

lining

6.5 cm (2½ in)

Figure 132

91

# Caring for Leather

After the time and effort you have put into making a bag, treat it with care. Never store it in a plastic bag. Leather must have a free current of air to 'breathe'. Empty the contents of the bag first if you want to hang it up; otherwise it may pull out of shape.

Keep it away from grease, especially if it is suede from which grease is extremely difficult to remove without marking the skin. A soft pencil rubber will erase light marks. If this is not successful, use the special cleaning pads on the market for these and minor stains or grease spots.

If you get caught out in the rain and your bag gets wet, hang it up to dry naturally — never near a fire or radiator.

Constant valeting is better than allowing dirt to become deeply engrained. Sponge grain leather gently with soapy water made up from a good quality toilet soap, leather soap or mild washing-up liquid (*not* detergent powder). Wipe it with a clean damp cloth, followed by a clean dry one.

Restore the nap on suede by brushing with a soft-bristled clothes brush or dry sponge. Never use a wire or stiff-bristled brush. For the best effect, hang the bag in a steamy bathroom first. Washable suedes must be treated strictly according to the suppliers' instructions.

Fibre dust, resulting from suede processing, often gets trapped in the leather's dense fibres and it may appear on the surface due to the friction of carrying; it can easily be brushed off.

# List of Suppliers

## UK

Gomshall Tanneries
Queen Street
Gomshall, Surrey
*Fashion suedes, including washable variety, and nappa leather (mail order or retail shop)*

J T Batchelor & Co
39 Netherhall Gardens
Hampstead, London NW3 5RL
*Quality leather, tools and fittings*

S Glassner
(Dept EOA)
68 Worple Road
Wimbledon, London SW19
*Tools, fittings, leather for accessories*

C & D Hudson
3 Roland Way
Higham Ferrers
Wellingborough, Northamptonshire
*Leather pieces sold by weight (mail order)*

B H Macready & Co
14 High Street
Brill, Bucks HP18 9ST
*Fashion skins of high quality*

John P Milner Ltd
67 Queen Street
Hitchin, Herts
*Skins, tools, linings and patterns*

G Tanners Ltd
Bridgehaugh Mill
Selkirk, Scotland TD7 5DR
*High quality pigskin leather*

U-duit
Church Street
Ripley, Derbyshire
*Dyes, tools, punches, belt shapes*

C W Pittard & Co Ltd
Sherborne Road
Yeovil, Somerset
*Grain leather and suede, gloving suede and glacé, in a range of colours*

David E Jacobs Ltd
263-5 Hackney Road
London E2
*Pigskin suede in range of colours, aniline vealskins*

Strong & Fisher Ltd
Rushden, Northants
*Suede and grain leathers, suedalope*

Connolly Bros (Curriers) Ltd
39-43 Charlton Street
Euston Road, London NW1
*Clothing leather sides and suede butt splits*

Rookes Leather Stores
Clemens Street
Leamington Spa
*Handbag leathers, skins or offcuts*

Dryad
Northgates
Leicester, Leics
*Handicraft leathers and tools (mail order)*
also 178 Kensington High Street
London W8 *(retail shop)*

Craftsmith Shops
branches in Hemel Hempstead,
Richmond, Slough, Exeter,
Southend-on-Sea and Nottingham
*Handicraft leathers and tools*

W H Peel & Co Ltd
Greenford
Middlesex
*Manufacture Chartwell True Sew dressmakers pattern guide paper, which is generally available through haberdashery departments and Singer sewing shops*

## USA

United Shoe Machinery Co Ltd
140 Federal Street
Boston, Mass
*Clothing leathers and tools*

A C Products
422 Hudson Street
New York
*Leather equipment and tools*

Tandry Leather Company
8117 Highway 80 West
Fort Worth, Texas
*Clothing leathers and equipment*

## AUSTRALIA

Leather House Grossman Pty Ltd
80 Campbell Street
Sydney, NSW
*Spanish suedes, glove leather and chamois*

Porter & Co Pty Ltd
Leather & Handcraft Supplies
203 Castlereagh Street
Sydney, NSW
*Calfskin, kidskin, pigskin, handcraft tools and accessories*

Platypus Manufacturers Pty Ltd
Cnr Tenterden Road &
Margate Street
Botany, NSW
*Garment nappa leather*

Reynolds Tanning Co Pty Ltd
13 Wilson Street
Botany, NSW
or Wallace Way
Chatswood, NSW
*Suede and grain leathers, chamois, and tools*

Mace-Lace Pty Ltd
Leather & Handcraft Supplies
8 Mollison Street
West End, Qld
*Modelling hides, calfskin, kidskin, pigskin, tools*

Basnett Garland Pty. Ltd.,
Leather & Grindery Merchants
47 King Street
Perth, WA
*Hides, suedes, chamois, tools and accessories*

Bulley & Co
Leather Merchants
380 Elizabeth Street
Melbourne, Vic
*Modelling hides, calfskin, suede, chamois, and tools*

Wingfield Hide Curing Co
Plymouth Road
Wingfield, SA
*Leathers, tools and accessories*

A size 18 sewing machine needle is generally used in Australia, and the adhesives recommended for use are: *Selleys Aquadhere, Duall 88* and *Standford 450 Stainless*

NEW ZEALAND

Classic Decor Ltd
PO Box 126
Thames Street
Napier
*Sheepskin products*

Glendermid Division of Michaelis
Bayley (NZ) Ltd
PO Box 944
192-6 Castle Street
Dunedin
*Clothing suede, bark tan, side leather for bags*

Outdoor Centre Ltd
PO Box 38017
282 Jackson Street
Petone
*Tooling leather, bag suede, embossing sets, dyes, rivets and belt buckles*

Pacific Leathers (NZ) Ltd
Commission Tanners
PO Box 870
Mersey Street
Pandora, Napier
*Garment suedes and nappa leather*

Waitaki Leather
PO Box 78
Oamaru
*Leather, suede and woolskins (mail order)*

94

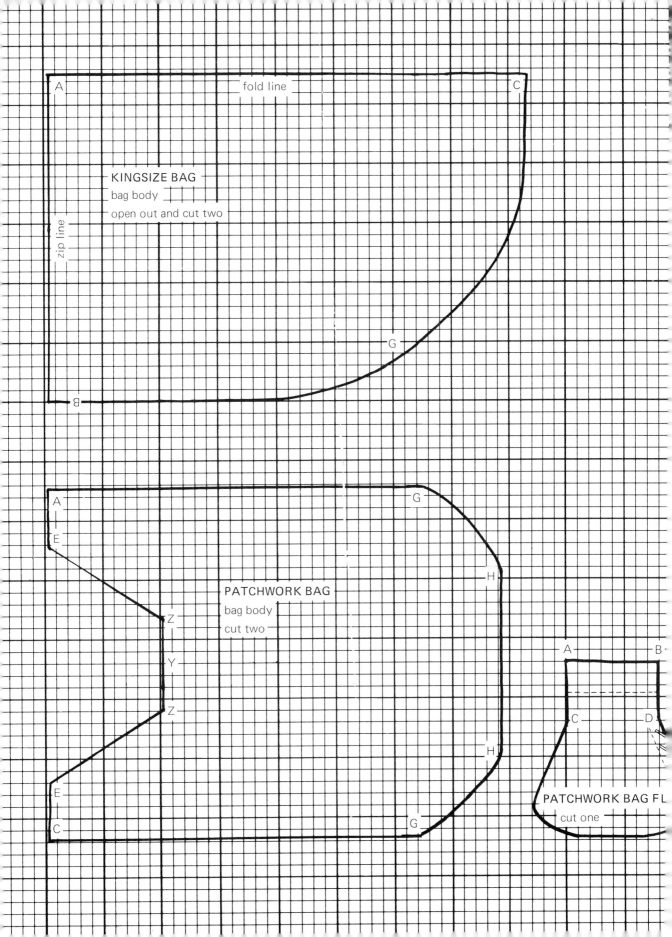

KINGSIZE BAG
bag body
open out and cut two

fold line

zip line

A

C

B

G

PATCHWORK BAG
bag body
cut two

A
E
Z
Y
Z
E
C

G

H

H

G

PATCHWORK BAG FL
cut one

A

B

C

D

# ndex